A YEAR'S SUPPLY

"Take heed, prepare, watch, and be ready."

Barry G. and Lynette B. Crockett

A Year's Supply is an urgent, practical, and simple guide to help you and your family prepare a year's supply of food, clothing, fuel, and other basic commodities to promote greater self-reliance, family preparedness, and provident living.

Barry Crockett holds an Associate of Applied Science Degree in Mobile Emergency Care (Paramedic) from Weber State College, a Bachelors Degree in Communications, and a Masters Degree in Health Education, both from Brigham Young University. Lynette Crockett attended Brigham Young University and Utah Technical College and is a mother and homemaker.

Library of Congress Catalog Card Number:
88-71201
ISBN 0-915131-88-9

First Printing September 1988
15 14 13 12 11 10 9
Publishers Press, Salt Lake City, Utah
Printed in the United States of America

Cover Photo: Electrical storm over Oklahoma City, Oklahoma
(Photo by National Severe Storms Laboratory)

On any given day some 44,000 thunderstorms rage around the world, with approximately 100 lightning strokes hitting the earth per second.

Additional copies may be ordered at $11.95 each plus $2.00 postage and handling by sending check or money order to:
Barry Crockett
P.O. Box 1601
Orem, Utah 84057

TABLE OF CONTENTS

PREFACE

A fundamental part of an individual or family becoming self-reliant is in acquiring and maintaining at least *a year's supply* of food, clothing, fuel and other items one may consider necessary for his wellbeing. Furthermore, it is essential that individuals and families develop the skills and resources required for self-reliance in the absence of commercially available products for an extended period of time.

Home storage works best when it is part of a family preparedness effort that includes education, career development, money management, health care, and emotional support. It is part of a sensible way to meet the ordinary requirements of day-to-day living.

It has been said "without food, nothing else matters." However, despite repeated admonitions from many Church leaders over the past 50 years, and in light of today's world conditions, about 97 percent of Church members still are not prepared with a year's supply of food, clothing and fuel.

One of the biggest obstacles is apathy. We live in an affluent society where nearly every service imaginable is at our fingertips or merely a phone call away. Many of us have become accustomed to this "room service." We shop for groceries every day or two at a corner market with as many as 6,000 different foods to choose from to satisfy our pampered appetites, and cannot fathom a situation where these goods and services would be unavailable. To many people, having to rely on some sort of "storage" seems intriguing, even amusing, if not downright fanatical.

Another force that discourages many from preparation is expense. It is difficult to spend our thought, energy, and money *now* to prepare for rainy days which may not come for some time, particularly when our everyday needs are great.

Others contend they have no room for storage, the food spoils, or that they don't like to eat such plain-tasting food. Still others argue that a substantial storage would be taken away or that they would be asked to share, thereby depleting their year's supply.

Though excuses are plentiful, every family and individual must face the problem of choice and the task of arranging priorities in regard to acquiring a year's supply. Failure to make the hard but essential choices required will inevitably lead to the day when the time for preparation is past, and one must face bitter-cold reality.

The purpose of this book is to encourage those who feel the need to prepare a year's supply as counseled by Church leaders, yet are unsure how to go about it. I hope this book will also challenge those who feel no need to prepare, or who feel that, should difficult times come, the government, the Church, or perhaps a provident neighbor will come to the rescue.

Having a year's supply of food, clothing, fuel and other basic necessities will give us peace of mind and a feeling of security in knowing we can provide for our own (and hopefully others) in times of need.

Barry Crockett

The most violent of all storms is the tornado. With rotating winds of up to 300 miles an hour, more than 700 tornadoes each year slash their way through cities and towns in every state in America, and many parts of the world. Making a noise like a jet squadron, a tornado leaves a path of almost complete destruction of everything in its path.

Some large tornadoes persist for hours, with paths up to a mile wide and hundreds of miles long. Usually the funnel moves — along with the parent thunderstorm — in an easterly direction, at speeds of up to 70 miles per hour. Tornadoes can occur at all times of the year and at any time of day or night, but are most likely in the spring and summer and in the afternoon and early evening. Its strike points cannot be predicted.

In this photograph by Dr. Eric Lantz, a killer tornado strikes Tracy, Minnesota, on June 13, 1968. The tornado traveled 13 miles along the ground, claiming nine lives, injuring over 100, and destroying much of the town. Residents had seven minutes' warning of the approaching tornado.

WHAT AND HOW MUCH TO STORE

Enough people have eaten for a long enough period of time that some conclusions on what to eat can be drawn from experience. Every individual does not like the same foods. Each family member should have some input into planning what foods to store. A simple, sensible rule is to store the foods that you normally eat if they provide an adequate diet. This rule will ensure that family members will eat the food that is stored and will ensure that stored food will be consumed within the shelf life period. **"Store what you eat, and eat what you store."**

Your **first priority** for storing foods should be **the basics—the life-sustaining core products—wheat, dry milk, sugar, salt and vitamins/minerals.** Give **second priority to fruits and vegetables**, stored in dried, home-canned, commercially-canned, or freeze-dried forms. Finally, store other food items that are normally eaten by the family, such as eggs, cheese, and meats. How much and what kinds of food to store will depend on where you live, what is available for storage, what you normally eat, your usual activities, your health, age, occupation, climate, your individual tastes, the size and ages of your family, and finally the extent to which you are going to store other foods. Most of these variables are built right into your everyday diet.

Most home food storage programs involve growing and preserving food at home from gardens and orchards. Generally, these sources provide a major portion of foods to the storage program between June and October. Home meat supplies are most commonly obtained in the fall during when wild game seasons occur and following pioneer traditions of slaughtering domestic animals during the cooler months to take advantage of natural refrigeration.

Surprisingly enough, the traditional family tends to eat the same foods in a rather erratic pattern throughout the year. This may border on boredom, but we basically eat what we like and can afford. Following are some suggestions for matching your storage needs with your usual needs:

- Work with your normal menu. Plan out a typical menu for a two-week period. Multiply the quantity of the basic ingredients in each meal by 26 (the number of two-week periods in a year). Then, tally all ingredients by commodity. The resulting list will show you which commodities you need in what amounts to feed your family for a year.

- You may prefer to use two menu sets—summer and winter—to take advantage of seasonal variations. In this case, multiply quantities of ingredients by 13.

- If you find it difficult to work with a full year's planning at once, you may want to apply a similar technique for a month at a time. Plan a two-week menu and buy double quantities of everything. Building a supply a month at a time can also be easier on the family budget.

- When shopping, buy two items for storage when you buy one item for current use.

- Keep a list of the main dishes, salads, vegetables, and desserts that you serve regularly. Most families have between 30 and 60 main dishes.

- Go through all your favorite family recipes and divide them into breakfast, lunch, dinner, beverages, breads, and snacks/desserts. Add up the quantities of basic ingredients that you would need for a year.

- Ask each family member to list four or five of his or her favorite breakfast, lunch, and dinner menus to help determine your needs.

- In storing a year's supply of non-food items, try going through each room in the entire house and yard as a family and writing down everything that's used regularly which you periodically need to replace or replenish. Prioritize this list beginning with non-food items that you family cannot do without.

- Go through the home writing down everything that uses electricity. In the event that there may possibly be no electricity for an extended period of time, determine how that appliance may be substituted, or, if it is really necessary, how it can be converted to battery or manual power. (Store lots of batteries.)

- Take advantage of case lot sales and other sale items. (Sale items are not always wise buys for long-term storage. Some goods may already have been stored for a long time. Check each item you purchase for an expiration date or a do-not-sell-after date. If they are coded, ask the store manager for an interpretation.)

- Buy fresh produce in season for the least expensive cost. Many farmers are happy to give away bushels of slightly bruised fruit. The bruises can easily be cut out before canning.
- In obtaining your one year supply, consider neighborhood group buying plans, barter organizations, grocery co-ops, wholesale grocers, grain mills, feed stores, and farmers.
- In summary, the principles for what to store are:

    1. Store what you are **accustomed** to eating.
    2. Store a **variety** of foods.
    3. Store foods that are **readily available** and **not too costly.**
    4. Store foods that supply all the nutrients needed in a **balanced diet.**
    5. Store only the **highest quality** or grade of food in the **best containers.**

SUGGESTED BASIC FOOD STORAGE FOR ONE YEAR:

Source: "Essentials of Home Production & Storage," published by The Church of Jesus Christ of Latter-day Saints, Salt Lake City, Utah (1978), p. 10.

Grains (wheat, rice, corn, or other cereal grains) — **300 lbs/person**

Nonfat Dry Milk — 75 lbs/person

Sugar or Honey — 60 lbs/person

Salt — 5 lbs/person

Fat or Oil — 20 lbs/person

Dried Legumes — 60 lbs/person

Garden Seeds

or

Fresh Taro
Sweet Potato
Pigs
Chickens
Fish

Above amounts are estimated for an average adult. They supply 2300 calories per day.

SUGGESTED BASIC FOOD STORAGE FOR ONE YEAR:

Source: "Having Your Food Storage and Eating It, Too" by Ezra Taft Benson Institute, Brigham Young University, Provo, Utah, p. 2.

Suggested Combinations for Yearly Requirements per Person		
Energy and Building Wheat 300 lbs (136 kg)	Rice or 370 lbs (168 kg)	Corn or 370 lbs (168 kg)
Building and Energy Dry Milk 50 lbs (23 kg)	Dried Fish or 50 lbs (23 kg)	Beans or 90 lbs (41 kg)
Energy and Protective Fruit or Vegetables* Fresh (Home Garden) 370 lbs (168 kg)	Pickled, or Canned, Bottled 370 qts (336 kg)	Dried or 90 lbs (41 kg)

*365 vitamin and mineral tablets *and* 100 lbs (45 kg) of sugar or honey or 35 lbs (16 kg) of fats in some form can be substituted for fruits and vegetables. Store extra water for use with dried foods. 5 lbs (2 kg) of salt and other seasonings may be necessary to make the food palatable.

SUBSTITUTES FOR THOSE WHO LIVE IN TROPICAL OR SEMITROPICAL CLIMATES
Source: Ensign Magazine

- Tropical and semitropical climates offer opportunities not available in the temperate zones. In the tropics, year-round gardens with a wide variety of fruits and vegetables are possible. The cereal grains can be replaced by taro, manioca, or sweet potatoes, all of which can be left unharvested for a considerable length of time and can thus be stored in the ground. Powdered milk can be replaced by fish, poultry, or hogs.

- Since the high temperatures of a tropical climate shorten the shelf life of stored foods, such commodities should be rotated through a period of several months rather than the year period recommended for a temperate climate. All foods should be stored in the coolest possible location. Dried foods are susceptible to high humidity and must be kept dry.

These familiar yellow and black civil defense signs identifying shelters are now faded; few list capacities, and many point to buildings soon to be demolished or no longer standing. Once stocked with food, water, sanitation and medical supplies, most of these shelters were intended to protect large numbers of citizens from radiation (not blast), while providing the necessities of life for about two weeks.

In reality, if hundreds or thousands of traumatized or injured people were to use these shelters, it would take only a couple of hours before it would become unbearable. The choking dust from the dirt floors and the stench from inadequate sanitation would be overwhelming.

WATER

☐ **Minimum of 14 gallons per person.**

• Water. People and livestock drink it, plants use it, and drains are flushed with it. Without water, there could be no life. Water is the single most abundant substance in the body, making up 50 to 60 percent of a person's weight. It is the most essential of all nutrients. **A person can live for many days without food but just a few days without water**. It is second only to air in importance to life. Water aids the entire digestive process. It dissolves substances so they can be transported throughout the body, and it carries away waste products. It also plays an important part in muscle contraction, nerve impulses and temperature control. It's recommended that we drink at least **six to eight glasses of water each day**.

• Because many types of disasters could cut off or contaminate water for short or extended periods of time, the Church and U.S. Government recommend water storage of one (1) gallon per person per day for two weeks (14 gallons for two weeks). This is absolutely essential and is a bare minimum, considering water usage in U.S. homes runs about 65 gallons per person per day.

Water storage containers may include:

☐ 5-gallon heavy duty plastic container with spigot to dispense the water (weighs 42 pounds when full).

☐ 6-gallon mylar water storage bags. Impermeable to odor, gas, and light. Contained in a cardboard box for easy stacking. Durable.

☐ 55-gallon heavy duty polyethylene plastic barrel or drum, with siphon pump and wrench to remove the cap. (Weighs 400 pounds when full.) Drums are also available in various sizes between 5 and 55 gallon.

☐ 2-liter plastic soda pop containers with screw-on lids.

☐ Thermos type containers.

☐ 1-gallon size glass jugs (padded with newspapers).

☐ "One way" mayonnaise jars (padded).

☐ Water can be "canned" in regular canning jars and processed for 20 minutes. (Re-pack in cardboard box and pad with newspapers.)

• Bleach bottles are not recommended for water storage. (Water may eventually become toxic.)

• 1-gallon milk containers are biodegradable and thus are not suited for long-term water storage.

☐ Short-term emergency water containers include a trash bag which has been placed in a pillow case or burlap sack, a bathtub, or a trench dug in the ground and lined with plastic.

Other sources of emergency water include:

☐ Hot water heaters. (Turn off the power source before draining.)

☐ Soft water tanks.

☐ Toilet tanks (not bowls), provided no chemical purifiers or disinfectants have been added.

☐ Waterbeds (king size has 200 gallons). Purify according to manufacturer's directions, otherwise use water for non-food purposes.

• Vinyl plastic waterbeds and bleach containers are not intended for long-term water storage for drinking. They may leach undesirable chemicals into stored water.

☐ Liquid in canned fruits and vegetables and fruit juices.

☐ Beverages.

☐ Melted ice cubes and melted snow.

☐ Large aquariums.

☐ Swimming pools.

☐ House pipes.

☐ Solar collectors.

☐ Solar stills (refer to Boy Scout fieldbook for directions on how to construct one).

☐ Lakes, rivers, ponds, creeks, ditches, and wells.

☐ Rainwater.

Water purification methods and equipment include:

☐ Filtering through layers of clean linen, nylon, or cheesecloth.

☐ Boiling water for 5-10 minutes (safest method).

☐ Adding 2-4 drops of household bleach (with four to six percent hypochlorite solution) to each quart of water, letting it stand for 30 minutes.

☐ 2% tincture of iodine (3-6 drops per quart of water).

☐ Iodine water purification tablets (unopened shelf life of 3-5 years). Follow the directions on the bottle.

☐ Halazone water purification tablets (unopened shelf life of two years). Follow the directions on the bottle.

• Water purification devices are available and may be useful; however, some gadgets are sold claiming they can "purify any water" and should be avoided.

• No home method of water treatment can guarantee safety of water but only reduces the risks involved.

• Fill containers to the top so there is no airspace and store in a cool, dark location, away from petroleum and insecticide products, away from strong odored food or perfumed products, and away from direct contact with concrete.

• Be sure all family members know where to find safe water, how to purify water, and the location of the home's main incoming water valve, so that they can shut it off to prevent entrance of contaminated water, if so directed.

• Store as much water as possible—more than the bare minimum (especially in desert and hot climates) and rotate or change the water every year. (Label with date rotated.)

• **Important Note:** Drink available water until your thirst is satisfied instead of trying to stretch the supply.

• Water with nuclear fallout particles in it is unsafe to drink until filtered and purified; however, the actual nuclear irradiation of water does not render it unsafe to drink.

During a hurricane, drinking water is of prime importance. You need enough for the duration of the hurricane, perhaps two or three days, plus a sufficient amount to cover any subsequent shortage due to broken water mains or contamination. Fill the bathtube and any other usable containers with drinking water. Before the hurricane strikes, turn off the water and follow utility advice on what to do about service lines. This way you can use water already in the pipes without fear of contamination.

Hurricane Carol, Crescent Beach, Connecticut, August 1954, United Press International photo.

WHEAT

☐ **300 pounds of wheat or other whole grains should be stored for each family member for a year's supply.**

- Consider the following when buying wheat:

    1) Buy **dark hard winter** or **dark hard spring** wheat. The best bread wheats in the world are produced where the winters are cold, the summers are fairly warm, and precipitation is adequate.

    2) Buy **number 2 grade or better** (not less than 58 pounds of wheat per bushel).

    3) **Protein** content should be from **12-15 percent**. (The effect of protein deficiency is most serious in children between the ages of one and six. It affects both physical and mental development.)

    4) **Moisture** content should be **10 percent or less.**

    5) The wheat should be **clean and free from living insects and foreign matter.** (The supplier should be willing to verify low moisture, protein content, cleanliness, and absence of living insects.)

- After purchase, the wheat should be placed in a sturdy, moisture-proof container. The best container for wheat storage is a five-gallon airtight metal container with a tight-fitting double-friction lid. (Seal is the same as a paint can.) These will hold about 35 pounds of wheat and can be stacked to save space. Sturdy polyethylene buckets with tight fitting lids are also acceptable for wheat storage. Don't store wheat directly on concrete floors. Keep cool and dry and away from steam, water pipes, unvented clothes dryer, wet clothes, etc.

- Since there may already be insect eggs present in the wheat which may hatch in due time, the stored wheat should be checked periodically for signs of insects. If infestation is found, several options may be considered. The degree of infestation may determine which you choose. Highly infested wheat, which appears to be covered with insect shells, contaminated with fine debris (excreta), and slowly crawling with insects, should be discarded if replacement is available. Such wheat may safely be used for animal or fowl feed. In times of emergency or with lower infestation levels, the wheat may be treated in a number of ways:

    1) It may be placed in a roasting pan or on a deep cookie sheet at a wheat depth of not more than two inches and placed in the oven at 200 degrees F. for one hour. Killed insects will dry out if left open to the air in a dry climate and may be removed by dropping the wheat in front of a fan or a moderate wind to blow away the debris while catching the grain in a large container. This should be done prior to subsequent storage.

    2) If the wheat is stored in an airtight container, it may be treated with dry ice. Remove all the wheat, except for one to two inches, from the container. Drop a piece (not pulverized) of dry ice (one-fourth pound per five-gallon container) in the container and pour the wheat on top of it. Place the lid on, but not tightly, for five to six hours; then tighten the lid to be airtight. Leave the wheat for at least one week; then use fan or wind to clean as suggested above.

    3) Place the entire container of wheat in a freezer at 0 degrees F. and leave it there for five to six days. Then remove it, allow it to dry, and clean as above.

- Work whole wheat and other whole grains into your family's diet gradually to prevent potentially serious digestive problems.

☐ **A good hand-powered wheat grinder or mill is absolutely essential.** Metal grinders are easier to use than stone grinders. (Some electric grinders can be converted to bicycle power.)

- Grind only enough flour to be used in a week's time for greatest freshness and nutrition. Whole wheat flour should be stored no more than six months and white flour no more than 12 months, and only in metal, airtight containers located in a cool, dry location.

- Store bread in original wrapper in a breadbox or refrigerator. Use within five to seven days. Bread keeps its freshness longer at room temperature than in the refrigerator. In hot, humid weather, however, bread is better protected against mold in the refrigerator than in the breadbox. Breads will retain their good quality for two to three months if frozen in their original wrappers and stored in the home freezer.

☐ White enriched flour.

The parching summer drought of 1988 proved to be the worst drought since the depression of the 1930s. Scorching temperatures often exceeding the 100 degree mark day after day, and the absence of rainfall most of the growing season, brought devastation to America's farmlands. As much as 35 to 40 percent of grain crops were destroyed, unequalled in magnitude for over half a century. Drought conscious consumers flocked to stores in a panic and were met with higher prices and shortages on many commodities.

Successive severe droughts often lead to famine conditions. Most recorded famines have resulted from widespread crop failures caused by a number of factors, including:

(1) Lack of water (drought), often followed by dust storms and loss of seeds; (2) Various types of diseases, such as fungus blights or pests, such as locusts. (3) Disruptions in farming operations due to war and civil disturbances. (4) A combination of factors hitting both crops and farmers as a result of large natural disasters, such as floods and earthquakes. Most of the major famines of the last two centuries have been a result of weather problems.

In this photo farmers in the American Midwest examine their grain crop. In the United States, less than three percent of our population produce most of our domestic food needs. Never before in the history of man have we ever had the necessary of depending on so few people to produce our food.

Top photo courtesy of Ezra Taft Benson Institute, Brigham Young University.

OTHER GRAINS

☐ **The 300 pound per person grain requirement for a year's supply should ideally include a variety of grains.**

- Cereals or grain crops such as wheat, oats, barley, rye and rice are grown for their edible seeds.

- Enriched grains, especially whole grain products, are important sources of the B vitamins, magnesium, iron and fiber. Examples of foods included in this group are whole grain and enriched breads, biscuits, muffins, waffles, pancakes, cooked and ready-to-eat cereals, cornmeal, flour, grits, macaroni and spaghetti, noodles, rice, rolled oats, barley, bulgar, and corn and flour tortillas.

- Following are some examples of various grains you may choose to store:

☐ Oats.

☐ Oat groats. High fat and protein. Oat and rye flours can be used as a substitute for wheat flour for people with allergies.

☐ Rolled oats (old-fashioned)—Used in cooked cereals, cookies, etc.

☐ Rolled oats (quick)—Cook faster, produce finer textured cereals and cookies.

☐ Rye—Stores well, used widely in Northern Europe in breads, porridges, and as meal.

☐ Rolled rye flakes—Used in granola mixes, breads and hot cereal.

☐ Triticale—A cross between rye and wheat, higher in protein than either rye or wheat, usually mixed with other flours for milder, sweeter flavored bread. Triticale can also be sprouted.

☐ Corn (field)—Used for flour and meal in cornbreads and tortillas.

☐ Cornmeal (yellow)—Ground yellow corn, used for cornbread and cereal.

☐ Popcorn—Stores well. Used as popping corn or ground into meal for cornbread.

- Popcorn "old maids" can be eliminated by running ice cold water over the kernels before throwing them into the popper.

☐ Barley (hulled, pearled)—Used in casseroles, soups, and beverages; stores well.

☐ Millet—Stores well, used for casseroles, porridge, and soups. Millet has an egg-like flavor.

☐ Pastas.

☐ Spaghetti.

☐ Elbow macaroni.

☐ ABC pastas—Alphabet noodles, used in soup and stew.

☐ Shell pastas—Used in soup, stew, salad, and casserole.

☐ Soup mix—Usually contains white rice, split peas, lentils, pearled barley, and ABC pastas. Stores well; just add flavoring.

☐ Rice.

Lengths:

- *Long* grain rice is distinguished because its length is four to five times its width. The grains are clear and translucent. The grains remain distinct and separate after cooking.

- *Medium* grain rice is about three times as long as its width. This type is less expensive than long grain rice. This is due to the fact that it requires a shorter growing season and produces a higher yield per acre. It is also easier to mill than the long grained variety.

- *Short* grain rice is only one and a half to two times as long as it is wide. It is generally the least expensive of the three lengths.

Kinds:

With five different kinds of rice to select from, it is important to be able to distinguish between the different varieties available.

☐ *Brown rice* is the whole, unpolished grain of rice with only the outer fibrous, inedible hull removed. Brown rice requires more water and longer cooking time than white rice. It has a delightful, chewy texture, with a distinctive nut-like flavor. (Cooks in 45 minutes.)

☐ *Regular milled white rice* is rice from which hulls, germ, outer bran layers and most of the inner bran are removed in the milling process. The grains are bland in flavor and are fluffy and distinct when cooking directions are followed. (Cooks in 15 minutes.)

☐ *Parboiled rice*—sometimes called processed or converted rice—has been treated to keep some of the natural vitamins and minerals the whole grain contains. It has been cooked before milling by a special steam pressure process. It requires longer cooking time than regular milled white rice, but after cooking the grains are fluffy, separate and plump. (Cooks in 25 minutes.)

☐ *Pre-cooked rice*—quick type—is completely cooked. It needs only to stand in boiling water to be ready for serving. Cooking this product will result in a gummy, indistinguishable mass. (Cooks in 5 minutes.)

☐ *Fortified or enriched rice*—This product is a combination of highly fortified rice with ordinary milled rice. A coating of vitamins and minerals—thiamine, niacine, iron, and sometimes riboflavin—is used to fortify rice. This coating adheres to the rice and does not dissolve with ordinary washing or cooking.

☐ *Wild rice* is not rice at all but the seed of a wild water grass found around the Great Lakes region. It is much more expensive than the types of rice described above. Many Americans have discovered this rice and developed a taste for it. The demand for it is almost greater than the supply.

• Do not wash rice before cooking or rinse it after cooking. Rice is one of the most sanitary foods. Rice grown and milled in the U.S. is clean. Nutrients on the surface of the rice are washed away if it is washed or rinsed before cooking.

• Do not use too much water when cooking rice. Any water drained off means wasted food value. Too much water makes soggy rice. Too little water results in a dry product.

• Do not peek when cooking rice. Lifting the lid lets out steam and lowers the temperature.

• Do not stir rice after it comes to a boil. This breaks up the grains and makes the rice gummy.

• Do not leave rice in a pan in which it is cooked for more than five to ten minutes or the cooked rice will pack.

• **Note on rice storage:** Uncooked milled rice (white, parboiled, and precooked) keeps indefinitely without refrigeration. Because of the oil in its bran layers, brown rice has a shelf life of only about six months. Refrigerator or freezer storage is recommended. Cooked rice may be stored in the refrigerator for up to one week or in the freezer for six months.

• Purchase only clean, insect-free, dry grain products (10-12 percent moisture or less) from a reputable miller. Store grains in metal airtight, five-gallon square cans that have a seven-inch diameter opening at the top and a friction lid. Well-made rigid plastic containers would be satisfactory. Avoid storing any grain in an open container. Store in a clean, cool, dry place, off the floor (preferably 18 inches) and away from damp areas. Rotate the supply.

• Flour should never be stored by apples, onions, potatoes, etc., as it will take up their flavors.

• Exotic treatment to prevent insect infestations in stored grain, such as bay leaves, chewing gum, salt, ten-penny nails, or chanting words and phrases are effective only when no insects are present in the food to begin with!

Bountiful, Utah was the sight of more devastation, just a day after the massive mudslide in Farmington, Utah. High up the steep slopes of Rudd Canyon east of Farmington, millions of gallons of water, mud and debris came crashing down onto the neighborhoods below. Most residents were sleeping when the power suddenly went off as the wall of water wiped out a nearby power station. Police ordered an immediate evacuation of several neighborhoods, warning residents of the approaching wall of water. Families scrambled out from their homes in the black of the night, with no electricity. Though no one was seriously injured, the flash flood washed one home away and damaged 50 others.

Here, emergency workers attempt to reinforce undermined dikes as surging floodwaters rip through the center of a residential neighborhood. Bountiful, Utah, May 1983.

NON-FAT DRY MILK/DAIRY PRODUCTS

☐ **75 pounds of non-fat dry milk per person for one year.**

- Milk and dairy products provide most of the calcium in our diet. They also supply vitamin A and protein. Most milk on the market has vitamin D added to it. Milk comes in many forms: whole, skim, low-fat, evaporated, buttermilk, and non-fat dry milk. Milk products include yogurt, ice cream, ice milk, and cheese, including cottage cheese. The various levels of fat in milk products allow for many individual choices in the diet.

- **Every adult** needs at least **two 8-ounce servings of milk** or other foods high in calcium per day. Though bones stopped growing long ago, calcium is still being removed from and replaced in the bones. Proper intake of calcium throughout adult life is important. The average American consumes about 557 pounds of dairy products in one year (fresh milk equivalent).

- Non-fat dry milk is a wholesome dairy product made from fresh milk. Only the cream and water are removed. It still contains the calcium and other minerals, the vitamins, natural sugar and high quality protein that make liquid milk such a valuable food. Non-fat dry milk, or powdered skim milk, does not have as much fat and is somewhat lower in calorie content than whole milk (dried) and will store much longer.

- Many dairy products can be made from powdered milk, such as reconstituted milk, cottage cheese, yogurt, cream cheese, and hard cheeses.

- Powdered milk may be purchased in both instant and regular forms. There is no nutritional difference between the two forms, and the storage life is equivalent.

- **Buy only "extra" grade** (the best of three grades). "Extra" grade contains four percent or less moisture. It should have been dried using a **"low heat spray process."** It should ideally also have been **fortified with vitamins A and D.** Lower quality powdered milk will develop an "off" flavor sooner than high quality milk.

- Dry milk should be stored in a tightly covered container (metal, rigid plastic, or glass) and stored in a cool, dry, and dark location up off the floor. Dry milk **must be rotated**, even if you package and store it correctly. Dry milk will store well at 40 degrees F. for 36-60 months and at 70 degrees F. for 12-24 months. Dry milk will store for extended periods of time in a vacuum or in a nitrogen atmosphere.

- Learn to save money on milk. Mix a quart of milk made from powder and water with a quart of whole milk and refrigerate it overnight. Use that milk to drink and use powdered milk to cook with. Doing this will help you rotate the powdered milk properly.

- To flavor dry milk and make it more palatable try adding a little vanilla, honey, nutmeg, cinnamon, almond, cream or cream substitute, banana, or chocolate. Adding air to the milk by mixing it in a blender helps improve flavor, as does serving the milk **ice cold**.

- A free publication on powdered milk is available for the asking called *Nonfat Dry Milk*, by Flora H. Bardwell, Pub. No. EL-142, Utah State University, Extension Services, Logan, Utah 84321.

- Other dairy products you may choose to consider as part of your year's supply include:

☐ Canned evaporated milk (shelf-life about one to two years).

☐ Canned baby formula (shelf-life about one to two years).

☐ Powdered baby formula—This is a "whole" type milk (shelf-life about two years). Rotate.

☐ Cream substitutes (non-dairy creamer). Shelf-life one to four years if vacuum packed.

☐ Cheese spreads—Shelf-life one year.

☐ Brick cheese—If cheese is to be stored for a long period of time, wrap it in cheesecloth dipped in white distilled vinegar and place in a plastic bag. Secure the bag with a twist tie and refrigerate. Shelf-life is six months to one year. Cheese can also be frozen.

☐ Powdered cheese—Dehydrated form stores several years. Use it dry or mix it with liquid or oil. The texture and consistancy of the powder, dry or reconstituted, does not resemble fresh cheese, but it does add cheese flavor.

☐ Margarine—Storage life is up to one year if stored in a very cool location.

Butter—Flavor granules—These require only hot water to develop the flavor of melted butter. The granules can be used to flavor vegetables, pasta, soups and sauces. (Because butter flavor granules contain no fat, they cannot be used for sauteing or frying.)

Powdered butter (dehydrated)—Has a shelf-life of several years. Butter powder can be reconstituted to make a butter spread. It can also be used to flavor sauces and soups.

Dried eggs—Freeze-dried and dehydrated egg solids are prepared by removing 90 percent or more of the water from fresh eggs. Dried egg products are available as whole egg solids, egg white solids, egg yolk solids, and various blends. Store dried egg solids in airtight containers in a cool location. They have a shelf-life of about two to three years. Most dried egg products are nitrogen packed.

How parents and others help an axious and frightened child cope after a disaster may have a lasting effect on the child. After a disaster, a child is afraid of recurrence, or injury, or death. He is afraid of being separated from his family, and he is afraid of being left alone.

On June 13, 1976, President Spencer W. Kimball and Elder Boyd K. Packer were airlifted by helicopter to Rexburg, Idaho shortly after the Teton Dam failed. President Kimball offered words of encouragement and counsel to those whose lives were shattered by the devastating flood.

"Exercise your priesthood," he told the brethren. "Bless your wives and children and call upon the heavens for inspired words of comfort. Hold your family home evenings. Let your children talk about their fears and frustrations, and let your children have something to say about the rebuilding of the home." He said the family circle is very important. "Your family activities should be carried out as normal as possible. Don't change your family patterns, patterns to which your children have been accustomed." He also admonished the holding of family prayer every night and a blessing on each meal.

After President Kimball concluded his remarks, parents brought their young children onto the stand, and President Kimball graciously shook hands with each of them, even squeezing the small hands of babies.

From CHURCH NEWS, week ending June 19, 1976, page 3. American Red Cross photo.

☐ **60 pounds of sugar and/or honey per person for one year should be stored.**

- Sugars are high in calories and low in nutrients and are one of the most maligned of all foods. There is no scientific evidence that sugar is responsible for all the problems attributed to it. The main health hazards from eating too much sugar are a possible increase in dental caries and obesity.

☐ White refined granulated sugar—If stored in a cool, dry place in a sealed container, it will usually maintain its food value indefinitely.

☐ Brown sugar—Keep in containers with tight-fitting lids. Unlike white sugar, it should be kept moist, or it will harden.

☐ Powdered sugar—Keep powdered sugar dry and store in containers with tight-fitting lids.

☐ Corn syrup—If the syrup crystalizes after long storage, place the container in a pan of hot water to melt the crystals. It stores well in a sealed container placed in a cool, dark, dry location.

☐ Pure crystalline honey (honey that has no water added)—Properly ripened and stored at room temperature, it will store indefinitely. Honey is more expensive than refined beet or cane sugar. Honey contains about 400 calories per pound less than refined sugar and is about twice as sweet as refined sugar.

- About 80 percent of extracted honey by weight is sugar, mostly in the form of simple sugars, which are easy to digest because they are already in the form that can be absorbed by the body. Most of the remaining weight is water. There are, in addition, small amounts of protein, minerals, and vitamins. (The mineral and vitamin differences between honey, brown sugar and white sugar are negligible. Neither honey nor brown sugar is significantly better than white sugar.)

- Flavor, aroma, and color of honey vary with the kind of flowers from which the bees gather the nectar to make the honey. As a rule, the lightest colored honeys are the mildest, such as sweetclover, clover, or alfalfa honey. Probably the darkest honey produced is buckwheat honey.

- The greatest share of extracted honey is sold in liquid form, but crystallized honey is becoming increasingly popular. Honey in crystallized form may be called "creamed," "candied," "fondant," or "spread"; it has a fine texture, spreads easily, and doesn't drip.

- **Top U.S. Department of Agriculture grade of extracted honey is U.S. Grade A or U.S. Fancy.** Next is U.S. Grade B or U.S. Choice. The most important factor in the grading of honey is flavor with respect to the predominating floral essence or floral blend. Absence of defects ranks next in importance. Also considered, but to a lesser extent, is clarity—that is, freedom from air bubbles, pollen grains, or other fine particles.

- Creamed honey may be kept at room temperature or in the refrigerator. Keep in the refrigerator if the temperature of the room is very warm. Creamed honey may partially liquefy if stored at too high a temperature.

- Honey kept for many months may darken slowly and become stronger in flavor but will still be usable.

- Honey may crystallize as it gets older or if kept at refrigerator temperatures or lower. Crystallization does not injure the honey in any way. To bring crystallized honey back to liquid form, place the container of honey in a pan of warm water until the crystals disappear. If further heating is necessary, raise the container of honey off the bottom of the pan by putting a rack under it and set the pan over low heat. Be careful not to overheat; too much heat causes the honey to change color and flavor.

- Honey may be used, measure for measure, in place of sugar.

- The Honey Association recommends that **infants under one year old should not be given honey because it is a raw product and may contain bacteria.**

- Other products in the sugar category you may wish to store include:

☐ Jams and preserves.

☐ Flavored gelatin.

☐ Powdered drink mixes.

☐ Sweet toppings.

☐ Syrups.   ☐ Candy.

☐ Pudding mixes.   ☐ Soft drinks.

SALT

☐ **5 pounds per person should be stored for one year.**

- Table salt is composed of sodium and chloride. One teaspoon of salt contains two grams of sodium. Sodium is a vital nutrient, playing an important role in maintaining blood volume and pressure by attracting and holding water in the blood vessels. Salt is needed by the body for enzyme reactions and keeps balance of acids and bases in the body. It also helps in the absorption of other nutrients, including carbohydrates. However, a little sodium goes a long way. Most Americans eat two-four times more sodium than they need. But if the kidneys are functioning properly, excess sodium should be excreted. **A safe and adequate intake is about 1.1 to 3.3 grams of sodium daily.** One teaspoon of salt equals two grams of sodium.

- Salt may be used with drying to improve storage time (as with fish) or with water to reduce spoilage (as with vegetables). Wash away excess salt before using the food.

- About five pounds of iodized salt per person will fill the requirement for one year. **In hot climates the amount needed may be as much as ten pounds.** Pickling salt may also be stored for bottling pickles and rock salt for making ice cream. Salt stored in a dry, cool, dark location in a sealed plastic or metal airtight container will keep indefinitely.

The total number of known active volcanoes is 850. The largest eruption in the United States was Mt. Saint Helens in Washington state. On May 18, 1980 a blast 500 times greater than the 20 kiloton atomic bomb that fell on Hiroshima, broke out the whole north side of the mountain. An avalanche of lava flowed out at a speed of 250 mph, destroying 100 square miles of forests and leaving 66 persons dead or missing. Photo courtesy of Federal Emergency Management Agency.

FAT OR OIL

☐ **20 pounds of fat or oil per person should be stored for one year** (1 gallon equals 7 pounds).

• Soybeans, flax, safflower, sunflower, and caster beans are examples of crops which are grown primarily for their oil. Soybean oil, for instance, is used in thousands of ways, but cooking oil and margarine are common uses.

☐ Cooking oil (vegetable).

☐ Shortening/shortening powder.

☐ Butter (fresh and dried).

☐ Margarine/margarine powder.

☐ Mayonnaise.

☐ Salad oils and dressings. (Dried mixes are available.)

• Fats supply concentrated energy and are a source of fat soluble vitamins (A, D, E, and K). Fat also composes part of the structure of cell membranes and helps to cushion body organs.

The hurricane season is between June 1 and November 30, and hurricanes are most likely to strike along the Atlantic and Gulf coasts. Hurricanes can be dangerous killers, provoking incredible destruction to persons and property. If you live in a coastal area, be prepared at the start of each hurricane season. Check your supply of boards, tools, batteries, non-perishable foods, and other equipment such as flashlights, first-aid kit, fire extinguisher, and battery-powered radio.

Pictured is Biscayne Bay as a hurricane whips spray across North Bayshore Drive's retaining wall. Miami, Florida, September 1948. Miami Daily News photo.

DRIED LEGUMES AND NUTS

☐ **60 pounds of dried legumes per person should be stored for one year** (Beans, peas, lentils, etc.).

- Beans provide an economical substitute for meat or other animal protein. Beans contain the highest protein content of all commercial seed crops. Beans are a good source of several B vitamins, as well as iron, calcium and magnesium. Beans are also an excellent source of starch and fiber.

- Dry beans are available in several forms—packaged in transparent packages, loose, or canned. The following are important factors in selection:
  1. Bright, uniform color. Color will vary with the variety of beans, but loss of color usually indicates long storage time.
  2. Uniform size. Uniformity of size will result in a more evenly cooked product since small beans cook faster than large beans.
  3. Freedom from defects. Cracked seed coats, foreign material, and pinholes caused by insects are signs of a low quality product.

  About one-third of all dry beans are officially inspected. Federal grades are generally based on shape, size, color, damage and foreign material. The packaged beans, which are on the grocery shelf, are normally the highest grades.

- Dry beans are an easily stored food. They should be kept in a tightly covered, metal, glass, or plastic container in a dark, dry, and cool location. The quality should be good for many years when stored under these conditions. Older beans will require longer soaking and cooking periods than freshly harvested beans, especially in dry climates.

- Varieties of beans:
  ☐ Navy Beans—Navy beans are also known as pea beans, a small white bean used in neavy bean soup, baked beans, casseroles and ethnic dishes. A large portion of the crop is used in canned beans and tomato sauce.

  ☐ Pinto Beans—The pinto bean is a variety of the red kidney bean which was first cultivated by the Indians of South and Central America. The pinto bean is grown in Southeastern Utah and Southwestern Colorado. It is used in Mexican dishes, such as refried beans.

  ☐ Kidney Beans—The kidney bean is large, red, and kidney shaped. They are frequently used for chili con carne and in salads, main dishes and casseroles.

  ☐ Black Beans—Black beans are also known as turtle beans and are used in Oriental and Mediterranean cooking. A rich, thick soup is made with black beans in the Southern United States.

  ☐ Lima Beans—There are two classes of lima beans—large seeded, or Fordhook type, and small seeded, known as baby limas. In the southern part of the United States, the lima bean is called butter bean.

  ☐ Chick Peas—Chick peas are also known as garbanzos in Spanish-speaking countries. Chick peas have a nut-like flavor and keep their shape well when cooked. Chick peas are used on salads and in casseroles and soups.

  ☐ Black-Eyed Beans—Black-eyed beans are also known as black-eyed peas or cow peas in different areas of the country. They are primarily used as a main dish vegetable and are traditionally served on New Year's Day in the South as a token of good fortune during the new year. They are small, oval-shaped, and creamy white with a black spot on one side.

  ☐ Split Peas—Split peas are green and yellow. In grocery stores, split peas come cleaned in one-pound packages. Large quantities in bulk might also be available in specialty shops. Split peas are commonly used in soups.

  ☐ Lentils—As the name implies, the lentil looks like a double lens. Lentils are dried on the plant and go through a number of processes to remove any extraneous plant materials. They always need to be looked at carefully before cooking. Lentils are grown in the United States and come in various shades of brown. Almost all are grown at an altitude over 2,000 feet in Washington and Idaho.

☐ **Soybeans**—Used as a meat extender. They have a mild flavor, are high in nutritional content, and have a high oil content which limits shelf-life (two-three years).

- Dry soybeans may be purchased year-round and are prepared for eating in the same ways as other dry beans.

- Soybeans can be sprouted for salads or served as a vegetable.

- Soybean milk, prepared from dry soybeans, may replace cow's milk in most recipes and can be used as a beverage.

- Soybean curd is prepared from soy milk and may be purchased fresh, canned, or as an instant powder.

- Soy sauce, a fermented product made from soybeans, is used as a seasoning, especially in Oriental foods.

- Soybeans are also a valuable source of oil, flour, and grits.

- Textured vegetable protein (TVP) is a vegetable protein made from soybeans, but its texture is similar to that of meat. When used with meat, TVP absorbs the flavor and cannot be distinguished from the meat. It can be bought as unflavored or flavored (beef, ham, bacon, or chicken). Shelf-life is two-three years.

- **Nuts** — Whole nuts keep better for long storage than chopped or broken nuts, and unroasted nuts keep better than roasted ones.

- Freezing nuts: Freeze shelled, unsalted nuts in their own sealed bags or in an airtight container. They will keep from six months to one year, depending on the age, condition and type of nuts.

- Vacuum-packed nuts: Unopened containers should be used within six months to one year. Keep them in a cool, dry location.

- Unshelled nuts: These store well for up to six months in a cool, dry place. Pour them into strong mesh bags. Hang the bags from the ceiling in a storeroom. Or place the nuts in perforated containers to allow air to circulate around them.

- Peanut butter stores well for about four years in unopened containers kept in a dark, cool, and dry location.

- Popular varieties of nuts you may wish to keep in your year's supply include:

☐ Almonds (6 calories per nut).

☐ Cashews (10 calories per nut).

☐ Peanuts (5 calories per nut).

☐ Walnuts (18 calories per nut).

☐ Pecans (10 calories per nut).

☐ Brazil nuts (24 calories per nut).

☐ Macadamia nuts (18 calories per nut).

America's number one weather-related killer is the flash flood. Flash floods now cause an average death toll of over 200 persons and property damage of more than one billion dollars each year. Across the nation flash floods most often strike at night, with the peak month being July.
Flash flood rescue operations, Rockville, Maryland, July 1975. Photo courtesy of National Oceanic and Atmospheric Administration.

VITAMINS AND MINERALS

☐ **365 tablets per person.**

- Vitamins are needed by the body only in very small amounts, but as the word indicates, they are **vital to the normal functioning of the body.** They are "helpers" and "regulators" in many body processes. Megadoses of vitamins are potentially harmful to the body.

- Minerals are also required by the body in very small amounts. Like vitamins, minerals work with other nutrients as helpers and regulators in the body. As with vitamins, you should avoid taking megadoses of minerals and trace elements.

- **It is recommended that 365 vitamin or vitamin/ mineral tablets be stored for each family member to** help compensate for possible deficiencies in the diet due to a lack of a variety of foods, vitamins lost during food processing, storage, and preparation. Vitamins and minerals come in tablet form, chewables, and liquid, to meet the needs of family members of all ages. Shelf-life is about three-five years if stored in a cool, dry and dark location. Consult your doctor.

- Despite careful food planning, **women may still need an iron and calcium supplement**, particularly if they are pregnant. Storage of iron and calcium should be carefully considered.

☐ High quality protein supplement. Buy only the best quality available. (Storage life is about one year.)

Nuclear explosions cause intense light (flash), heat, blast, and initial nuclear radiation, which occur immediately. In addition, explosions that are on or near the ground create large quantities of dangerous radioactive fallout particles, most of which fall to earth during the first 24 hours. Pregnant women and small children are most at risk from radiation.

"In the event of a Soviet first strike, it would take 2.8 minutes for the first missiles to hit the United States. The attack, from start to finish, would take 30 minutes."* The current American position is one of extreme vulnerability to a Soviet first strike against our strategic nuclear deterrent forces. Following such an attack, fallout radiation and the effect of direct strikes is not expected to pose the major concern. Direct effects would include a total world economic collapse and loss of critical systems in the United States such as communications, transportation, fuel production and distribution, and many medical/surgical services. The biggest problem would be a widespread famine resulting from crop loss for 12 to 24 months.

United States Department of Defense photo.

*"The Soviet Challenge," Dr. E. Eugene Callens, Jr., Regional Representative. Address delivered at Brigham Young University, July 15, 1987.

MEALS — READY-TO-EAT

- Meals-ready-to-eat is the U.S. military's current field ration for all ground troops. They were introduced in 1979 as **the latest, best tasting, longest storing food that could be produced which needed no refrigeration to keep an army fed in the field.** A full meal MRE consists of an entree, supplementary dish, some sweet, and an accessory pack that contains drinks, salt and pepper, spoon, etc.

- MRE retort pouches contain the food and are comprised of three layers of metal and plastic that will not puncture easily, is easy to open, and will not leave a metallic taste even after years of storage. A retort pouch is filled with food, sealed, and cooked with superheated steam to cook the food and kill all bacteria while retaining nutrients.

- Stored in a cool location, retort foods will store for seven to ten years, although they should be rotated every six years to maintain optimal quality. Since they are fully cooked, retort foods may be eaten cold or heated first. **During storage, do not freeze retort foods or expose to high heat.**

One of the primary things a family should do in preparing for emergencies is to evaluate which threats may affect the family and to prioritize and examine those threats. Each family should then develop an emergency response plan that can be immediately implemented. For example, in Salt Lake City, weather extremes must be considered. In 1864, Mark Twain observed, "I stood on Main Street in Salt Lake City and while the sun was shining on my back, I could see a snow storm developing in the purple mountains to the east." Salt Lake City is subject to harsh winter storms producing large accumulations of snow, dense fog, and frequent power outages. In the summer, severe thunderstorms and lightning are the primary threats, spawning at least two tornadoes each year, as well as hurricane force winds from the east canyons.

From those same canyons, major flooding, massive landslides and mudslides are common. Salt Lake City is also overdue for a high intensity earthquake, increasing the likelihood of any one of several dams failing east of the city. In addition, Salt Lake City has the usual dangers such as transportation accidents involving hazardous or toxic materials, fires, and pipeline accidents. Finally, the ominous nuclear threat is an eventuality that we all must deal with, regardless of where we reside.

Photo courtesy of Salt Lake City Convention and Visitors Bureau.

SPROUTING

☐ **Store several pounds of your family's favorite sprouting seeds.** Store them in airtight containers in a cool, dry, and dark location.

• Sprouting grains and lentils at home is an inexpensive way to have a continually fresh supply of vitamin-rich sprouts for soups, salads, sandwiches, and Oriental dishes.

• Popular choices include alfalfa, mungbeans, garbanzo beans, whole green peas, lentils, radishes, and triticale. (Soybean sprouts should be cooked, and corn sprouts simply do not taste good.)

• Most seeds can be sprouted; however, avoid sprouting tomato or potato seeds, both of which are toxic. Also **don't sprout seeds which have been treated with insecticides.** And lastly, occasionally a fuzzy mold may develop on the sprouts. Such mold can be toxic, and these spouts should be discarded.

• Place ¼ cup of washed seeds in a quart-size wide-mouthed jar. Add one pint of lukewarm water. Put cheesecloth or a piece of nylon stocking over the mouth of the jar, securing with a rubber band or a jar ring. Let stand overnight, then drain off the water. Turn jar upside down. Turn the jar on its side and shake so the seeds separate and spread along the side of the jar. Keep the jar in a warm, dark cupboard or closet. Rinse sprouts twice a day in lukewarm water, drain and spread sprouts along the side of the jar again. In three-five days, your one-inch sprouts are ready to refrigerate to keep fresh for eating.

A mud-encrusted survivor is evacuated to an awaiting rescue helicopter in the wake of one of the deadliest volcanic eruptions in all of recorded history. Late in the evening on November 13, 1985, the long dormant volcano Nevado del Ruiz erupted. The volcano sent a steaming, mile-wide avalanche of grey ash and mud down the mountain, burying the town of Amero, near Bogota, Colombia. The 50-foot high wall of molten lava, melted snow, and mud traveled about 30 miles an hour down the mountain, depositing a layer of mud and ash 15 feet thick, entombing most of its 23,000 victims. The volcanic eruption was roughly equivalent to the A.D. 79 explosion of Mount Vesuvius, which destroyed the cities of Pompeii and Herculaneum. At the time of this volcano, Latin America was still painfully coping with the aftermath of the Mexico City earthquake, occurring just eight weeks previous, which claimed 10,000 lives.
Time Magazine cover photo. Used by permission.

FOOD EQUIPMENT ITEMS

- ☐ Canning jars, lids, and rings.
- ☐ Ice cream maker with hand crank.
- ☐ Bottle opener.
- ☐ Non-electric can opener.
- ☐ Cooking utensils that are fire safe.
- ☐ Paper or plastic plates, cups, and utensils.
- ☐ Insulated ice storage chest and reusable ice packs.
- ☐ Good cookbooks on how to use basic food storage.
- ☐ Aluminum foil.
- ☐ Oven wrap.
- ☐ Plastic wrap.
- ☐ Freezer wrap.
- ☐ Waxed paper.
- • If you're out of paper plates, line regular dishes with plastic wrap, waxed paper or foil to be discarded after eating.
- ☐ Zip-loc type plastic bags.
- ☐ Twist ties.
- ☐ Paper napkins.
- ☐ Paper towels.
- ☐ Rubber dishwashing gloves.
- ☐ Fishing supplies.
- ☐ Hunting gear and ammunition.
- ☐ Manual egg-beater.
- ☐ Non-electric food processor.
- ☐ Flour sifter.

- ☐ Breadboard and rolling pin.
- ☐ Several bread loaf pans.
- ☐ Small food grinder for preparing baby food.
- ☐ Seed sprouting kit.
- ☐ Grease pencils to mark processing and purchase dates on jars and cans.
- ☐ Fire-safe pots and pans.
- ☐ Cast iron Dutch oven.
- ☐ Thermos jugs.
- ☐ Iron stand for cooking in the fireplace.
- ☐ Non-electric meat grinder.
- ☐ Food and oven thermometers.
- ☐ Asbestos gloves to work with a Dutch oven in and around the fire.
- ☐ Toasting forks.
- ☐ Long-handled fork, spoon, tongs, and spatula for turning and stirring food near the fire without getting burned.
- ☐ Skewers for roasting hot dogs, etc. (Try using a cleaned pitchfork for a skewer.)
- ☐ Stiff metal brush for cleaning barbeque grills after use.
- ☐ Commercial kettle cooker.
- ☐ Extra grills for cooking. (A cooking grill placed over a bed of coals in a wheelbarrow, children's wagon, or over a large flowerpot or even an inverted metal garbage can lid can make a satisfactory cooking device.)
- ☐ Griddle.

STORAGE CONTAINERS

- **Metal storage cans or heavy plastic containers with airtight lids are preferred.**

- Label all storage containers with the contents and purchase date. If nothing else works, try a grease pencil.

- Plastic trash bags have been chemically treated and should not be used to store food in.

- Only plastic containers that have been approved by the FDA should be used to store food or water. If you are unsure, ask the manager at the place of purchase or inquire of the manufacturer.

- Use unbreakable containers if possible.

- Water is best stored in unbreakable plastic containers rather than glass.

- Put padding such as newspaper or foam between canning jars (or other jars) and store them in their original cardboard boxes for safety during an earthquake. These boxes should be lined with plastic sheeting to contain any breakage. This method also excludes light from the food.

- Do not stack storage containers which are breakable.

- Build sturdy storage shelves with a heavy wire or small piece of lumber attached to the front of each shelf to keep contents from falling in the event of an earthquake.

- Storage should not be in contact directly with the floor and especially concrete. Instead, put such storage on spaced lumber, i.e., pallets or pop crates, to allow circulating air under the storage to protect from rusting and moisture damage from "sweating" concrete and to reduce damage in the event of flooding.

- Leave foods in their original packages if possible. Instructions for preparing foods are often printed on the package. Place the packaged foods inside your long-term storage containers. If you must remove foods from their packaging, cut off the instructions, wrap them in plastic wrap and keep them with the food.

- *Paper.* If there is much moisture in the surrounding air, the food can absorb it. Sugar, for instance, can go lumpy. Insects and rodents can easily chew through the paper. The food may also pick up odors from the air.

- *Cardboard.* Thick cardboard will reduce air exchange with the food and help to keep out odors but does not protect food completely from insects and rodents.

- *Polyethylene.* Plastic sacks can form an airtight seal that will prevent air exchange, but insects and rodents can eat through them.

- *Plastic.* Tight-fitting lids will prevent any air exchange, but determined rodents have been known to eat through heavy plastic containers. Generally, however, they are satisfactory.

- *Glass.* Besides bottled foods, bottles can be used for water, dry beans, macaroni, nonfat dry milk, and other such products. These containers are impermeable to air, insects, and rodents if lids fit tightly.

- *Metal.* Metal containers may be canisters, bins, or large storage cans, or cans of food from the store. If tightly sealed, metal can prevent any air exchange. It is insect and rodent proof. But in high humidity areas, metal can rust easily. If such is the case, all metal cans should be painted with a rust-retarding paint.

"The revelation to store food may be as essential to our temporal salvation today as boarding the ark was to the people in the days of Noah.

". . . Noah built his ark before the flood came, and he and his family survived. Those who waited to act until after the flood began were too late." (Ezra Taft Benson, October Conference, 1973.)

"It has been asked, and well might it be, how many of us would have jeered, or at least been privately amused, by the sight of Noah building his ark. Presumably, the laughter and the heedlessness continued until it began to rain—and kept raining. How wet some people must have been before Noah's ark suddenly seemed the only sane act in an insane, bewildering situation!" (Neal A. Maxwell, NEW ERA, January 1971.)

Pictured is the corner of State Street and North Temple, with the Church Office Building and Relief Society Building in the background. Despite attempts to re-direct the floodwaters by using thousands of sandbags and plastic sheeting, minor flood damage nevertheless resulted in lower levels of the Church Office Building.

May 1983, Salt Lake City, Utah.

- Keep food in the **driest** (less than 15 percent humidity) and **coolest** spot (usually the northeast corner of a home basement) and choose a **dark** area if possible. Keep a thermometer and humidity indicator in the storage room to monitor these factors.

- For optimal shelf-life and nutritional quality, **foods should be stored between 40 °-60 °F., with an upper limit of no more than 70 °F.** The lower the temperature, the longer the shelf-life. (Critical storage temperatures: 32 °F. — freezing; 48 °F. — insects become active; 95 °F. — fat melts.)

- For every 20 °F. increase in storage temperature, the optimal shelf-life of food is decreased by one-half.

- Store nothing on cement floors. Place slats of lumber between the cement and the storage to prevent sweating and rusting.

- Excessive dampness will rust cans or metal lids. If this condition becomes severe, leakage will occur, and the product will spoil. Freezing causes expansion of the product, and the jar lids may crack, or can seams may be stressed. This can lead to leakage and food spoilage. Avoid storage near steampipes, radiators, furnaces or kitchen ranges.

- Never store foods near petroleum products, household chemicals, or any strong-odored substances.

- **Store supplies in various locations in the house so if one part is damaged, you still have something left.**

- Keep food storage areas free of spilled food and food particles to help prevent insect infestations.

- If you live in a troublesome flood-prone area, you may need to keep your storage in the attic or upper level of the home.

- It is a good idea to have the lowest shelf in your storage room two-three feet off the floor in flood-prone areas.

- In tornado-prone areas, the southwest corner of the home basement is generally the safest location for storage.

- Foods can be stored in the following locations:
  - Basements
  - Insulated garages (may be too hot)
  - Attics (may be too hot)
  - Root cellars
  - Pits (storage type)
  - Freezers
  - Crawl spaces (may be too cold or humid)
  - Under beds and cribs
  - In chests of drawers
  - Footlockers
  - Trunks
  - Clothes closets
  - Cedar chests
  - In luggage
  - In bookcases
  - Food storage can be arranged as a foundation for a mattress or other furniture.
  - Space made available by family or friends can also be utilized for food storage.
  - In rented storage units.

- After the storage area and shelving are completed, the area should be carefully cleaned. Then spray the area with a household formulation of an approved insecticide, such as pyrethrum or malathion. Once the spray dries, cover the shelves with clean shelf paper before putting the food on the shelves.

- Nutrient content of foods depends on natural differences, control of deterioration, and handling techniques of food preparation, as well as preservation.

- Always obtain top grade food products for storage.

- Buy nitrogen packed foods whenever possible (for longer storage life and better quality, with no insect infestation).

- When foods are preserved by heating, as in home canning or commercial canning, the heating process is designed to destroy all normal spoilage bacteria that can grow under usual storage conditions and all bacteria capable of causing human harm. The products are called "commercially sterile" but are not always truly sterile.

- Canned foods will remain wholesome and usable for many years if cans are in good shape and not bulging.

- About two to five percent of food value is lost each year in canned foods stored under ideal conditions.

- Canned goods should be turned upside down every six months or so to prevent contents from settling.

- Keep all food covered at all times.

- Open food boxes or cans carefully so that you can close them tightly after each use.

- One of the **fundamental tenets of a successful storage program is the rotation of supplies** (1) to prevent spoilage and to minimize loss of food value and flavor and (2) to keep our taste buds acquainted with the foods we someday may have to depend upon.

- When we store foods too long, we run the risk of two things happening: (1) the color, flavor, odor, texture and appearance deteriorate to a level where people will not consume the food, and (2) nutrient deterioration may be severe enough to render the food an unreliable source of specific nutrients.

- Keep paper and pencil in the storeroom and record storage items you remove so you can take the list to the store to replenish the items.

- It is wise to check the storage area on a regular monthly basis.
  1. Check bulk grains for rodent and insect infestation.
  2. Make sure the food is being rotated properly.
  3. Remove bulging cans or unsealed packages and jars and dispose of them.
  4. Make sure the written inventory is accurately kept.
  5. Monitor the temperature and humidity.
  6. Check for water seepage and moisture damage.

Involve all family members in operating the system.

Immediately after an earthquake one must check for injuries, check for fires and gas leaks, and turn off utilities if necessary. It is also important to turn on a radio or television to get official emergency information and instructions. Remember also to restrict telephone use to true emergencies, stay out of damaged buildings, and prepare for aftershocks.

Residents in this and other homes narrowly escaped injury when giant boulders crashed down nearby mountains onto the small town of Challis (near Boise), Idaho, during a massive earthquake measuring 7.0 on the Richtor Scale. The earthquake claimed two lives and was felt in eight Western states and parts of Canada.

Idaho earthquake, November 1983. Deseret News photo by O. Wallace Kasteler.

27

COMMONLY STORED FOODS CHECKLIST

- **GRAINS (300 pounds of grain products recommended per person).**

☐ Wheat

☐ White rice

☐ Oats

☐ Corn

☐ Rye

☐ Barley

☐ Flour

☐ Cereal

☐ Popcorn

☐ Garden and sprouting seeds

- **PASTAS**

☐ Macaroni

☐ Noodles

☐ Spaghetti

- **MILK/DAIRY PRODUCTS (75 pounds of dairy products recommended per person.)**

☐ Non-fat dry milk

☐ Canned milk

☐ Condensed milk

☐ Dried eggs

☐ Dried cheese

☐ Brick cheese

☐ Cheese spreads

☐ Canned sour cream

☐ Non-dairy creamer

☐ Infant formula

- **JUICES/BEVERAGES (25 pounds of fruit juice recommended per person. 46 oz. = 2.6 lbs.)**

☐ Orange juice

☐ V-8 juice

☐ Grape juice

☐ Apple juice

☐ Cranberry juice

☐ Grapefruit juice

☐ Tomato juice

☐ Pineapple juice

☐ Plum juice

☐ Prune juice

☐ Apricot nectar

☐ Baby strained juices

☐ Soft drinks

☐ Soft drink mixes

☐ Punch crystals or concentrates

☐ Tang

☐ Kool-aid mixes

☐ Lemonade mixes

- **CANNED OR DRIED MEATS (20 pounds of meats recommended per person.)**

☐ Ham—Some canned hams require refrigeration.

☐ Beef

☐ Bacon

☐ Pork

☐ Fish

☐ Tuna fish

☐ Salmon

☐ Clams

☐ Shrimp

☐ Crabmeat

☐ Sardines

☐ Spam

☐ Treet

☐ Lunchmeat

☐ Sandwich spreads

- [ ] Deviled meats
- [ ] Vienna sausage
- [ ] Pepperoni
- [ ] Sausage
- [ ] Hamburger
- [ ] Corned beef
- [ ] Lamb
- [ ] Mutton
- [ ] Veal
- [ ] Chicken
- [ ] Turkey
- [ ] Beef jerky
- [ ] Venison jerky
- [ ] TVP – Textured Vegetable (soy) Protein

- **LEGUMES (90 pounds of legumes recommended per person.)**
- [ ] Beans
- [ ] Peas
- [ ] Lentils
- [ ] Sprouting beans and seeds
- [ ] Soybeans

- **NUTS**
- [ ] All kinds

- **FATS/OILS (20 pounds of fats/oils recommended per person.)**
- [ ] Butter
- [ ] Margarine
- [ ] Cooking oil
- [ ] Shortening
- [ ] Lard
- [ ] Peanut butter
- [ ] Mayonnaise
- [ ] Salad dressing

- **SUGARS (60 pounds of sugars recommended per person.)**
- [ ] Sugar (all forms)
- [ ] Honey
- [ ] Corn syrup
- [ ] Maple syrup
- [ ] Molasses
- [ ] Jello and puddings
- [ ] Hard candy, gum
- [ ] Jellies, jams

- **FRUITS (bottled, canned, or dried)**
  (The per person recommendation for fruits and vegetables is 90 lbs. dried or 370 quarts of bottled or canned, or 370 lbs. of fresh.)
- [ ] Peaches
- [ ] Pears
- [ ] Cherries
- [ ] Berries
- [ ] Applesauce
- [ ] Pineapples
- [ ] Apricots
- [ ] Fruit cocktail
- [ ] Apples
- [ ] Plums
- [ ] Tomatoes
- [ ] Currants
- [ ] Grapes
- [ ] Raisins
- [ ] Grapefruit
- [ ] Nectarines
- [ ] Coconut
- [ ] Mandarin oranges
- [ ] Olives
- [ ] Figs
- [ ] Prunes

- **VEGETABLES (fresh, canned, or dried)**

☐ Corn (Sweet corn loses up to 30 percent of its flavor in the first six hours after picking.)

☐ Peas

☐ Tomatoes

☐ Beans

☐ Green beans

☐ Potatoes

☐ Pickles

☐ Sauerkraut

☐ Asparagus

☐ Beets

☐ Hominy

☐ Mushrooms

☐ Okra

☐ Spinach

☐ Squash

☐ Pumpkins

☐ Sweet potatoes (yams)

☐ Carrots

☐ Broccoli

☐ Water chestnuts

☐ Rhubarb

☐ Peppers

☐ Rutabagas

☐ Salsify

☐ Turnips

☐ Celery

☐ Onions

☐ Parsnips

☐ Brussel sprouts

☐ Cauliflower

☐ Artichoke hearts

- **SOUPS (canned or dried)**

☐ All kinds

- **AUXILIARY FOODS**

☐ Baking soda

☐ Baking powder

☐ Cream of tartar

☐ Cornstarch

☐ Vitamins/minerals

☐ Iron supplement

☐ Calcium supplement

☐ Salt

☐ Instant yeast

☐ Crackers

☐ Cookies

☐ Marshmallows

☐ Pectin

☐ Plain gelatin

☐ Rennin tablets

☐ Pie fillings

☐ Chow mein noodles

☐ Instant breakfast

☐ Pancake mixes

☐ Hot roll mixes

☐ Cake mixes

☐ Casserole mixes

☐ Pie crust mixes

☐ Muffin mixes

☐ Pastry mixes

☐ Whipped topping mixes

☐ Pizza mixes

☐ Cookie mixes

☐ Pudding mixes

☐ Non-perishable pet foods

- **SPICES/CONDIMENTS/FLAVORINGS**

☐ Salt

☐ Pepper

☐ Cinnamon

☐ Nutmeg

☐ Onion salt

☐ Onion flakes

- [ ] Garlic salt
- [ ] Seasoned salt
- [ ] Ginger
- [ ] Chili powder
- [ ] Cloves
- [ ] Herbs
- [ ] Allspice
- [ ] Basil
- [ ] Bay leaves
- [ ] Celery salt
- [ ] Coriander
- [ ] Cumin
- [ ] Curry
- [ ] Dill weed
- [ ] Chives
- [ ] Ginger
- [ ] Marjoram
- [ ] Orange peel
- [ ] Oregano
- [ ] Paprika
- [ ] Poultry seasoning
- [ ] Cayenne pepper
- [ ] Sage
- [ ] Tarragon
- [ ] Thyme

- [ ] Turmeric
- [ ] Soy sauce
- [ ] Worcestershire sauce
- [ ] Vanilla extract
- [ ] Lemon extract
- [ ] Maple extract
- [ ] Almond extract
- [ ] Vinegar
- [ ] Mustard
- [ ] Ketchup
- [ ] Spaghetti sauce
- [ ] Barbeque sauce
- [ ] Steak sauce
- [ ] Liquid smoke
- [ ] Gravy mixes
- [ ] Salad dressing mixes
- [ ] Lemon, lime juice
- [ ] Sauce mixes (taco, enchillada)
- [ ] Bouillon cubes, granules (beef, ham, chicken, onion, vegetable flavors)
- [ ] Cocoa
- [ ] Chocolate syrup
- [ ] Chocolate chips (and other flavors)
- [ ] Baking chocolate (unsweetened)
- [ ] Protein supplement

Following the Mexico City earthquake, Mexican Red Cross rescue teams, as well as paramedic rescue teams from California, began to work round-the-clock clearing away the rubble to save lives.

Here, after hours of digging into twisted steel and broken concrete, in an attempt to trace a faint cry for help, rescuers locate a survivor.

Mexico City earthquake, September 1985. Photo courtesy of League of Red Cross and Red Crescent Societies.

SHELF-LIFE OF COMMON STORAGE FOODS

- **Shelf-life is defined as the period of time between slaughter or harvest and consumption.** Scientists determine the shelf-life of a food by storing it under carefully controlled conditions for a given period of time. During this storage period, measurements are made to monitor changes in two important parameters: (1) the quality of the food (i.e., color, flavor, texture, odor) and (2) the nutrients it contains (i.e., vitamins, protein, fat, water, minerals and carbohydrate).

- There are several important factors which influence shelf-life and would be important to consider in a food storage program. Temperature, humidity, packaging material, irradiation, the presence of insects and animals, availability of non-food chemicals, and formation of natural toxicants are just a few of the parameters which must be considered in establishing shelf-life recommendations.

- **The following recommendations were not made to establish how long food may be stored but instead to provide data for a sensible rotation system.**

- The information that follows lists the food item, type of packaging, and **approximate storage time (in months) at 40 °F.**

Item	Packaging	40 °F.
Almond paste	Can	36
Antioxidant compound, food service	Bag	60
Apple:		
Regular pack	Can	72
Pie style, dehydrated	Can	36
Butter	Can/jar	48
Sauce	Can	72
Baby food, strained	Jar	36
Dehydrated (instant)	Can	36
Dietetic pack	Can	66
Junior food	Jar	36
Juice	Can	60
Dehydrated	Can	60
Single strength	Can	60
Apricots:		
Regular pack	Can	60
Baby food, strained	Jar	30
Dietary pack	Can	56
Dried	Carton	24
Freeze, dehydrated	Can	24
Apricot nectar:		
Regular pack	Can	48
Freeze, dehydrated	Can	24
Asparagus	Can	60
Baby formula preparation	Can	24

Item	Packaging	40 °F.
Bacon:		
Sliced	Can	48
Sliced, irradiated	Can	48
Sliced, prefried	Can/flexible pkg	48
Bakery mixes	Can	48
	Bag/carton	12
Baking powder	Can	24
Baking soda	Carton	indef
Barley, pearl	Bag/carton	36
Banana, baby food, strained	Jar	24
Beans:		
Dried	Bag/carton	24
Green, baby food, strained	Jar	30
Green, regular	Can	60
Green junior food	Jar	30
Green dehydrated	Can	84
Kidney	Can	72
Lima	Can	72
Lima, dehydrated	Can	60
Sprouts	Can	48
Wax	Can	60
White, dehydrated	Can	48
White with pork in sweet sauce	Can	72
White with pork in tomato sauce	Can	60
Beef, liver, pork or veal:		
Baby food, strained	Jar	30
Junior food	Jar	30
Beef:		
Broth, baby food, strained	Jar	30
Chunks with natural juices	Can	60
Corned	Can	60
Diced, raw, dehydrated	Can	60
Flakes/shaped, raw, dehydrated	Can	60
With gravy	Can	60
Patties, dehydrated	Can	60
Beef steak, raw, dehydrated	Can	60
Beets:		
Baby food, strained	Jar	24
Junior food	Jar	24
Regular pack	Can	48
Berries, black, etc.	Can	40
Beverage base:		
Cocoa, liquid	Can	36
Cocoa, powder	Can	60
Imitation, liquid	Bottle	48
Powder	Envelope	60
Blueberries	Can	36
Cabbage:		
Cooked, dehydrated	Can	72
Raw, diced, dehydrated	Can	60
Candy:		
Caramel	Box	12
Coated (bridge mix)	Box	24
	Can	60
Hard	Can	60
Starch jelly	Box	24

Item	Packaging	40 °F.
Carrot:		
Baby food, strained.............	Jar	36
Junior food	Jar	36
Puree.........................	Can	72
Regular pack	Can	72
Catsup:		
Regular pack	Bottle	48
	Can	36
Dehydrated	Envelope/can	72
Cereal:		
Baby food, strained, barley	Container	24
Quick cooking	Carton	12
	Can	36
Ready to eat, prepared	Pkg	24
Sugar coated	Pkg	12
Cheese:		
Cheddar, processed.............	Can	60
Cottage, dehydrated	Can	24
Grated........................	Container	18
Processed, American, dehydrated..	Can	36
Cherries:		
Dehydrated	Can	48
Dietetic pack	Can	36
Maraschino	Jar	24
RSP (red sour pitted)	Can	24
Sweet, dark	Can	42
Sweet, light...................	Can	56
Chewing gum	Carton	9
Chicken:		
Dehydrated	Can	60
Regular pack	Can	60
Baby food, strained............	Jar	30
Chili con carne:		
Without beans	Can	48
Dehydrated, with beans	Can	60
Chili sauce	Bottle	48
Chocolate, cooking:		
Semi-sweet chips	Pkg	36
Unsweetened	Carton	48
Chocolate syrup, beverage	Can	60
Clams	Can	48
Cocoa, natural..................	Carton	36
	Can	60
Coconut, prepared:		
Sweetened.....................	Can	36
	Container	24
Unsweetened	Bag	24
Cookies.........................	Carton	6
Corn, cream and whole grain styles...	Can	72
Corn, dehydrated, LPPD, cooked		
or uncooked	Can	48
Corn chips	Pkg	1
Corn meal......................	Pkg	36
	Can	36
Crackers:		
Graham	Carton	4
Oyster, soda	Carton	6
Cranberry sauce..................	Can	48
Cream:		
Coffee type, 18 percent fat	Container	12
Whipping, 30 percent fat	Container	12
Substitute	Can/envelope	60
Whipping, dry	Can	8
Cream of tartar	Container	indef
Currants, dried	Carton	24
Custard, pudding, baby food,		
strained....................	Jar	15

Item	Packaging	40 °F.
Dessert powder:		
Gelatin, based, all flavors	Can	60
	Container/pkg	36
Starch, based, all flavors	Can	60
	Container/pkg	30
Instant, all flavors	Can	60
	Carton	30
Egg mix, dehydrated	Can	60
Eggs, whole, dry	Can	60
Emulsifier, bread and rolls	Bag/can	18
Figs	Can	48
Fish, dehydrated:		
Patties.......................	Can	60
Squares......................	Can	60
Flavoring:		
Imitation maple or vanilla	Bottle	indef
Nonalcoholic, lemon, orange,		
peppermint, rum	Bottle	24
Rye	Fiberdrum	12
Tablet, imitation maple or vanilla ..	Bottle	indef
Flour:		
Rye	Bag	30
Wheat, hard or soft	Can	48
	Bag	30
Food coloring	Bottle	indef
Food packet:		
Abandon aircraft...............	Can	60
In flight.....................	Carton	60
Long-range patrol	Case	84
Survival, abandon ship	Carton	84
Survival, aircraft, liferaft	Can	84
Survival, general purpose	Carton	60
Frankfurter	Can	60
Fruitcake	Box	10
Fruit, candied	Jar	12
Fruit cocktail	Can	56
Fruit mix, freeze, dehydrated........	Can	24
Fruit puree	Can	48
Fry mix, breading	Bag	24
Garlic:		
Dehydrated	Can	36
Dry	Box	5
Gelatin, plain, edible..............	Container	60
Grape juice:		
Dehydrated	Can	60
Single strength	Can	30
Grapefruit:		
Regular pack	Can	56
Juice, dehydrated (instant)........	Can	60
Juice, single strength	Can	48
Grapefruit — orange juice blend:		
Dehydrated	Can	60
Single strength	Can	48
Ham chunks.....................	Can	60
Hamburgers, without gravy	Can	60
Hominy:		
Grits	Container	36
Whole	Can	60
Honey, extracted	Jar	36
Horseradish, dehydrated	Bottle	36
Ice cream mix:		
Paste	Can	24
Powder	Can	36
Icing mix.......................	Can	60
Inhibitor, mold, bread and rolls	Bag	12
Jam, fruit	Can/jar	48
	Pkg	24

Item	Packaging	40 °F.
Jelly, fruit.......................	Can/jar	48
	Pkg	24
Lard, service style	Carton	12
Lemon juice, dehydrated	Can	60
Lime juice, single strength	Can	30
Luncheon meat	Can	60
Macaroni	Carton	48
Malted cereal syrup	Can	60
Margarine.........................	Can	60
Marmalade........................	Jar	48
Marshmallow......................	Container	12
Mayonnaise	Can/jar	10
Meal, combat, individual	Case	60
Meringue powder	Can	48
Milk:		
Chocolate (cocoa flavored)	Envelope	60
Chocolate, sterilized	Can	12
Dry, non-fat....................	Can/drum	60
Evaporated.....................	Can	24
Filled, dry, including chocolate	Can	24
Malted dry	Can	60
Whole, dry	Can	60
Whole, sterilized	Can	12
Mincemeat	Can	36
Molasses	Can	60
Monosodium glutamate	Container	indef
Mustard, prepared	Can/jar	36
Mushrooms	Can	56
Noodles:		
Chow mein	Can	6
Egg	Carton	36
Nuts:		
Shelled, roasted	Can	60
Unshelled	Bag	12
Okra	Can	48
Olives:		
Green	Jar	36
Ripe...........................	Can	36
Olive oil	Can	18
Onions, dehydrated................	Can	48
Orange juice:		
Dehydrated (instant)	Can	60
Single strength	Can	48
Parsley, dehydrated	Can	18
Peaches:		
Baby food, strained..............	Jar	30
Dietetic pack	Can	56
Regular pack	Can	60
Slices (freeze dehydrated)	Can	24
Peanut butter	Can/jar	60
Pears:		
Baby food, strained..............	Jar	33
Dietetic pack	Can	60
Freeze dehydrated	Can	24
Regular pack	Can	66
Peas:		
Baby food, strained..............	Jar	33
Black-eyed	Can	66
Dehydrated, cooked/uncooked....	Can	60
Dried..........................	Bag/carton	24
Green	Can	66
Peppers, green, dehydrated	Can	60
Pickles:		
Cucumber, cured	Jar	36
	Can	24
Cucumber, fresh pack...........	Jar	27
	Can	18

Item	Packaging	40 °F.
Mixed	Jar	36
	Can	24
Relish	Jar	36
	Can	24
Pie filling, prepared fruit, apple, cherry, peach	Can	36
Pimientos	Can	48
Pineapple:		
Dietetic pack	Can	48
Freeze dehydrated	Can	24
Juice, dehydrated	Can	60
Juice, single strength	Can	60
Regular pack	Can	60
Plums:		
Dietetic pack	Can	48
Regular pack	Can	56
Popcorn, unpopped	Can	96
	Carton	2
	Cello bag	24
Pork chops, raw, dehydrated	Can	60
Potato:		
Chips..........................	Pkg	1
	Can, air	4
	Can, nitrogen	24
Sticks	Can	36
Sweet	Can	56
Sweet, instant, dehydrated	Can	48
White	Can	56
White, dehydrated..............	Can	48
Prunes:		
Baby food, strained.............	Jar	15
Dehydrated/pitted (low moisture)..	Can	24
Dried..........................	Can	36
Dried, soaked...................	Can	24
Pumpkin..........................	Can	56
Raisins, dried	Can	36
Ration supplement aid station	Case	60
Rice:		
Instant	Carton	36
Milled	Bag	36
Parboiled	Container/bag	24
Salad dressing	Can/jar	8
Salad oil	Can	24
Salmon	Can	60
Salt:		
Celery, garlic, onion	Container	60
Substitute	Envelope	indef
Table..........................	Bag envelope	indef
Sauces, hot, kitchen, meat, soy or Worcestershire.................	Bottle	48
Sauerkraut	Can	36
Sardines	Can	48
Sardines in tomato sauce	Can	24
Sausage, pork, link	Can	60
Shortening compound:		
Bakery type	Can/cube	60
Deep fry, cooking type, fluid	Can	60
Deep fry, cooking type, plastic	Can	60
General purpose, regular	Can/cube	60
General purpose, high stability	Can/cube	60
Shrimp	Can	48
Shrimp, dehydrated	Can	60

Item	Packaging	40 °F.
Soup:		
Baby food, chicken, strained	Jar	30
Beef noodle, dehydrated	Pkg	48
Chicken, chunk, dehydrated	Can	60
Chicken, noodle, dehydrated	Can	60
	Pkg	48
Condensed	Can	48
Cream of onion, instant, dehydrated	Flexible pkg	24
Cream of potato, instant, dehydrated	Flexible pkg	24
Green pea, instant and simmer types, dehydrated	Pkg/can	24
Lima bean, instant, dehydrated	Can	60
Onion, dehydrated	Can	60
	Pkg	24
Ready to serve	Can	48
Tomato-vegetable w/noodle, dehydrated	Can	48
Vegetable, dehydrated	Pkg	24
Soup and gravy base:		
Beef flavored	Can/jar envelope	48
Chicken, flavored	Can/jar envelope	48
Ham, flavored	Can/jar envelope	48
Sour cream sauce mix	Can	24
Spaghetti	Carton	48
Spices, seasonings, herbs	Can	60
	Container	36
Spinach:		
Baby food, strained	Jar	30
Dehydrated, cooked	Can	60
Junior food	Jar	30
Regular pack	Can	56
Puree	Can	56
Starch:		
Corn, edible	Carton	60
Pregelantized edible	Can/bag	indef
Sugar:		
Brown	Carton	36
Confectioners	Carton/bag	36
Refined, granulated	Bag/can, envelope	indef
Sugar substitute	Envelope	indef
Syrup:		
Blended	Can	60
Maple syrup, imitation	Bottle/can	60
Tapioca	Carton	60
Tomato:		
Juice, concentrated 3 + 1	Can	36
Juice, single strength	Can	36
Paste, instant, dehydrated	Can	60
Paste, regular pack	Can	36
Puree	Can	42
Regular pack	Can	48
Topping, dessert:		
Dehydrated	Can	36
Tuna:		
Dehydrated	Can	60
Dietetic water pack, no added salt	Can	48
Oil pack	Can	60
Water pack	Can	48
Turkey:		
Dehydrated	Can	60
Regular pack	Can	60
Vegetable:		
Baby food, mixed, strained	Jar	30
Juice, single strength	Can	36
gar:		
Liquid	Bottle	48
Synthetic, dry	Flexible bag	24
Water	Can	indef
Wheat, base	Bag	48
Yeast, baker's, active dry	Can	6
Yeast food	Bag	48

During a tornado, homes disintegrate not because of low pressure causing them to explode, which is a myth, but because tornado force winds tear roofs away, causing the walls to fall down. Therefore, opening windows won't help. If you are in a house or building, go to the interior part of the house or building to the smallest room on the lowest floor. If you are outside in an automobile, abandon the automobile in favor of a permanent structure. If a permanent structure is not available or if you are out in the open outside of an automobile, you should find a ditch or depression that would permit you to get as low as possible and avoid the debris. (Federal Emergency Management Agency photo.)

STORING FRESH FRUITS AND VEGETABLES

- Many fruits and vegetables can be stored fresh. But the home gardener must gather them at proper maturity and observe correct temperature, humidity, ventilation, and cleanliness rules.

- Basements or outdoor cellars can serve as temporary storage for some produce. A cellar mostly below ground is best for root vegetables. It can be run into a bank and covered with 2½ feet or more of soil. Sometimes outdoor root cellars are made with a door at each end. Combining the outdoor storage cellar with a storm shelter in the event of tornadoes or other needs may be a satisfactory solution.

- Modern basements are generally too dry and warm for cool, moist storage. However, a suitable storage room may be built by insulating walls and ceiling and ventilating through a basement window. You may ventilate by extending a ventilating flue from half of the window down almost to the floor. Cover the other half of the window with wood and the outside openings of the ventilator with a wire screen for protection against animals and insects.

- Keep the room cool by opening the ventilators on cool nights and closing them on warm days. If properly cooled, the room temperature can be controlled between 32 degrees and 40 degrees F. during winter. To maintain the humidity, sprinkle water on the floor when produce begins to wilt. A slatted floor and slatted shelves will provide floor drainage and ventilation. A reliable thermometer is needed for operation of any home storage room.

- A cool corner in the basement, a back room of a small house with no basement, or a trailer may be suitable. One lady we know uses part of a closet built into the outside corner of a bedroom. It is also possible to adapt storage sheds in carports by insulating and proceeding as outlined earlier.

- Pits and trenches or mounds may be used for storage if a root cellar is not available or basement storage is impractical. Also, you may bury a barrel or drainage tile or galvanized garbage can upright, with four inches of the top protruding above ground level. This will keep potatoes, beets, carrots, turnips, and apples through winter. For convenience, place the produce in sacks or perforated polyethylene bags of a size to hold enough for a few days. Then you can easily take out fruits and vegetables as needed.

- Place the barrel on a well drained site and make a ditch so surface water will be diverted and not run into the container. A garbage can has a good lid, but for a drainage tile or barrel a wooden lid may have to be built. The lid should be covered with straw, and a waterproof cover of canvas or plastic placed over the straw.

- Requirements of fruits and vegetables differ. Controlled cold storage or refrigerated storage are best.

- Good references are *Storing Vegetables and Fruits in Basements, Cellars, Outbuildings, and Pits,* USDA Home and Garden Bulletin No. 119 and bulletins on this subject prepared by your State Extension service. Your county Extension office may have the bulletins. This office may also be able to tell you how to obtain plans for a fruit and vegetable storage room or a storm and storage cellar.

A quiet Memorial Day afternoon in Farmington, Utah turned into a nightmare as hundreds of thousands of tons of rock and mud roared out of the Wasatch foothills. The mud and water carried with it huge boulders and trees, swallowing up a dozen homes and severely damaging dozens of others. Residents had only a moment's warning to evacuate from the approaching 20 foot high wall of mud. Miraculously, no lives were lost.

Farmington, Utah, May 1983, American Red Cross photos.

CANNING AND BOTTLING

- **Canning is probably the most economical and practical method of preserving food at home.** Heat-processed foods that are sealed in a closed container, such as a glass bottle or a tin can, **can be stored from one to five years,** if stored in a cool, dry and dark location. Appropriate containers, equipment, and fuel are necessary for this process and may be expensive. Canning must be done in a steam or water bath and not in the oven.

- Selection of good sound fruits and vegetables is of paramount importance. The quality of canned fruits and vegetables will be no better than quality of the raw food used. For best flavor retention, preserve only those vegetables that are young, tender, and freshly gathered.

- Fruits and vegetables can sometimes be obtained inexpensively at the end of the growing season from orchards and farmers (bruised fruit or produce that is threatened by an impending hard frost or freeze).

- If you don't have reliable processing instructions, don't attempt home canning. If you have these instructions, read them before and during home canning and do not take short cuts or modify the instructions. Do not use processing instructions of neighbors or relatives; although frequently given with the best of intentions, they may contain modifications that are inadequate and dangerous. Remember that past safe history of a relative's processing procedure is no guarantee of future safety. Botulism doesn't always occur even in inadequately processed home-canned foods.

- Canning information can be found in many good resource materials. Commercial canning books, such as Kerr and Ball Blue books, extension and USDA bulletins, farm journals and seed catalogues.

- The following two publications contain excellent information on canning, freezing and drying and probably contain the most reliable information available on food preservation:

- *Ball Blue Book Home Canning Manual.*
  Ball Corporation
  Consumer Products Division
  Consumer Affairs
  345 South High Street
  Muncie, Indiana 47302

- *Kerr Home Canning Manual*
  Kerr Glass Manufacturing Corporation
  Sand Springs, Oklahoma 74063

- Commercial canning is done under tightly controlled conditions—careful sanitation, just the right heat and timing—but there are still limits to how long it will preserve food. There are several factors that limit the shelf-life of canned foods. First, cans can rust over time. When rust is deep enough, tiny holes open in the can that may let spoilage agents in. Shipping accidents—where cans fall or are crushed—also cause container problems.

  Then there's can corrosion. In all foods, but especially in high-acid foods like canned tomatoes, the food continually reacts chemically with the metal container. Over several years, this can cause taste and texture changes, and eventually lower the nutritional value of the food.

  High temperatures (over 100°F) are harmful to canned goods too. The risk of spoilage jumps sharply as storage temperatures rise. In fact, canned goods designed for use in the tropics are specially manufactured.

  And accidentally frozen canned goods left in a car or basement in subzero temperatures can present health problems. If the cans are merely swollen—and you're sure the swelling was caused by freezing—thoroughly cook the contents right away. You can eat or refreeze the cooked food. But if the seams have rusted or burst, throw the cans out.

- While extremely rare, botulism is the worst problem you can encounter in canned goods. Never use food from containers giving out possible botulism warnings—leaking, bulging, or badly dented cans, cracked jars or jars with loose or bulging lids, canned food with a foul odor, or any container that spurts liquid when you open it. **Don't even taste such food!**

  Seal the product in a plastic bag marked "Danger." To avoid leakage, sit it on a paper plate. Refrigerate it on a high shelf, out of the reach of children. A health official may want to examine it later.

- Store canned foods in a cool, clean, dry place. Temperatures below 70°F. are best.

- **Canned ham**—Store it in the refrigerator for use within six-nine months.

- **Low-acid canned goods**—Store in the cabinet for two-five years. Products: Canned meat and poultry, stews, vegetable soups (except tomato), spaghetti (noodle and pasta) products, potatoes, corn, carrots, spinach, beans, beets, peas, pumpkin.

- **High-acid canned goods**—Store in the cabinet for 12-18 months. Products: Juices—tomato, orange, lemon, lime, and grapefruit; tomatoes; grapefruit; pineapple; apples and apple products; mixed fruit; peaches; pears; plums; all berries; pickles; sauerkraut; and foods treated with vinegar-based sauces or dressings, like German potato salad and sauerbraten.

- **Boil all home-canned foods before serving**—First bring the food to a rapid boil. This brings out any tell-tale botulinum odors. Some botulinum bacteria produce gas you can smell.

  If the product smells all right, lower the heat and continue boiling the food, covered, for a second period: ten minutes for high-acid foods and 20 minutes for low-acid foods—meat and poultry products, peas, beans, and corn.

  The second boiling kills any botulinum toxin that might be present even though you can't smell it.

  Complete both boiling periods before tasting for quality or to add seasoning. But if a spoiled odor appears or the food is foaming or looks odd, throw it out without tasting.

CANNING EQUIPMENT:

☐ Boiling water bath canner—For processing acid foods. Height of kettle is important. Jars, when seated on rack, must be covered by one-two inches of water [25-51 mm], with an additional one-two inches of air space above to permit boiling.

- For fruits, tomatoes, and pickled vegetables, use a boiling-water-bath canner. You can process these acid foods safely in boiling water. For all common vegetables except tomatoes, use a steam-pressure canner. To process these low-acid foods safely in a reasonable length of time takes a temperature higher than that of boiling water.

☐ Pressure canner—Available in various sizes. Size should be related to needs of the family. Pressure canners may be obtained with either weighted or dial gauges.

- Use of a pressure canner for preserving low-acid foods is not new. Pressure canners for home canning were first marketed in the early 1900s. In 1917, the U.S. Department of Agriculture announced that use of a pressure canner at ten pounds pressure (240°F.) was the only safe method for canning vegetables. Today's recommendations are essentially the same.

- Trying to use a pressure canner obtained from garage, rummage, or auction sales or handed down to you from someone's attic may prove dangerous. You may not have any idea as to the care, handling, or storage of the canner. A manufacturer manual on care, use and replaceable parts usually is not available.

☐ Steam canner—Safe only for high acid foods. This method is designed to be used at home in the place of the boiling water bath. Research scientists at Utah State University and Brigham Young University have tested the steam canner and pronounce it safe and effective only for processing fruits, jams, pickles, tomatoes, and other high acid foods.

☐ Crock—A needed item when fermenting food, as in pickling. Crock should be clean and free of cracks. Glaze should not be chipped.

☐ Jar funnel—Commercially available funnels are made especially for canning. Funnel helps avoid getting particles of food on sealing surfaces of jar and aids in determining proper head space.

☐ Jar lifter—May be purchased where canning supplies are sold. Soft plastic coating prevents jars from slipping and wooden handles protect the hand from heat.

☐ Bubble freer—A plastic bubble freer, or a similar non-metallic utensil, is required to run down sides of filled jars to release air bubbles without damaging interior of jar.

☐ Jars—Standard home canning jars should be used. The size of the jar should be based on the needs of the family.

- Select standard canning jars made of tempered glass that can withstand high temperatures. The manufacturer's name or symbol in glass will identify the product. With careful handling, jars last an average of about ten years. Avoid using antique jars because there can be hair-line cracks not visible to the eye, causing jars to break.

- Use canning jars in sizes suitable for the product canned and your family's needs. Canning jars generally are sold in half-pint, pint and quart sizes with wide and narrow mouths. Large-mouth jars are convenient for packing such foods as whole tomatoes and peach halves. Quart jars are convenient for vegetables and fruits where your family has four or more members.

- "One-trip" jars, like the ones in which you buy commercially canned mayonnaise, peanut butter, or baby food, should not be used for home canning. Commercial jars are made to serve a single purpose only—to package food products. They are not meant to be reused for home processing. And often they are made for a food product that is packed cold and therefore may not be made to withstand the temperatures used in home canning.

☐ Lids—Standard lids from a reliable manufacturer of home canning supplies should be used. The manufacturer's directions should be followed carefully.

- Closures — Jar lids and rings come with new canning jars. The sealing compound of lids recommended for one use only will not hold a seal effectively after the first use. Screw ring bands may be reused if kept clean and dry in a protective container with a tight-fitting lid. Never use bands with rust or pried up or bent edges. If you have extra lids, store them protected in a dry, cool place.

☐ Spoons — A necessity for stirring, spooning, packing and lifting. Use wooden spoons for stirring and packing; slotted spoons for lifting. Accurate measuring spoons are essential.

☐ Knives — A variety of knives is necessary, including a good paring knife, a sharp chopping knife (butcher or French) and a vegetable peeler.

☐ Food brushes — Food to be canned must be carefully washed. Food brushes with stiff bristles facilitate this work.

☐ Saucepans — Occasionally needed to heat lids.

☐ Measuring cups — Both dry (metal) and liquid (glass) measuring cups should be on hand. Measurement capability should range from ¼ cup [60 mL] to 2 cups [480 mL].

☐ Jelly bags — Made from a thin fabric (usually cheesecloth) to help strain juice from softened fruit and pulp.

☐ Colander or strainer — Helps hold fruit or vegetables after washing. Excellent for draining.

☐ Tongs — Kitchen tongs are used for removing home canning lids from hot water and placing the lids on jars as each jar is filled.

☐ Scales — Essential for following recipes where ingredients are given by weight. Scale with capacity up to 25 pounds [11 kg] is desirable.

☐ Timer — Necessary for measuring processing times accurately by the minute.

- A wind-up timer should also be obtained for occasions when there is no electricity.

☐ Juicer

☐ Victoria-type food strainer. Essential for making applesauce, etc.

☐ Pit remover — For removing pits in cherries.

☐ Pectin, lemon or lime juice, ascorbic acid.

- **JAM AND JELLY EQUIPMENT**

☐ Water bath canner

☐ Jelly thermometer

☐ Timer

☐ Widemouth funnel

☐ Large, flat-bottomed kettle (8-10 qt.)

☐ Measures

☐ Measuring cup and spoons

☐ Food chopper or masher

☐ Long-handled spoon

☐ Colander

☐ Ladle

☐ Jar lifter

☐ Jelly bag and cheesecloth

☐ Jelmeter

☐ Canning jars and fittings

☐ Parafin wax

- It is a good idea to label each jar of food. The date that the food was canned should be included. Food that has been properly canned will keep indefinitely, but after a year some chemical changes do occur. For this reason, food that has been canned the longest period of time should be used first. The label might also include information on the type and variety of food that was canned, the recipe used, whether the food was hot or cold packed, and any additional information desired. This kind of information can help in the future to duplicate successes and eliminate failures.

"Now you probably have read of the terrible disaster in Idaho since our last conference. Brother Packer and I visited the scene of the disaster. A big dam burst and flooded many communities. The water that reached as high as 20 or 30 feet deep swished through the homes and the farms and the Church buildings and wreaked great damage. Thousands of head of cattle and other animals were destroyed. We were grateful that the warning came in the daytime when all people could be warned. I think only seven people lost their lives, but the destruction was terrible. We just mention that so that you will be prepared in this area. There are famines and dry periods. There are earthquakes and cyclones and divers problems that arise in the various parts of the country. The thing that pleased us was that our people were partly ready. Even though their own personal supplies were washed away, yet we had a surplus in our storehouses. And almost as soon as the word went out, our trucks were moving to Idaho filled with tons of relief commodities. Ricks College, which was just above the water line, was used for homes and for the feeding of the people. Beds were made all through the college, and tens of thousands of meals were supplied. When we visited the President of the United States recently, I told him, 'We are prepared.' The Lord said, 'If ye are prepared ye shall not fear.' (D&C 38:30.) Our Relief Society organizations and our bishoprics and our stake presidents all knew what to do. And the work went forward immediately while the nation was trying to get together and plan and organize. We want you to be ready with your personal storehouses filled with at least a year's supply. You don't argue why it cannot be done; you just plan to organize and get it done." (Spencer W. Kimball, Scandinavian Area Conference, Copenhagen, Denmark, August 1976.)

FREEZING

- **Freezing is one of the simplest and least time-consuming ways to preserve foods at home.** It keeps well the natural color, fresh flavor, and nutritive values of most fruits and vegetables. Frozen fruits and vegetables are ready to serve on short notice because most of the preparation they need for the table is done before freezing.

- Freezing, like canning, does not improve food quality. Top quality fresh fruits and vegetables are essential for premium frozen products. Quality factors include a suitable variety for freezing, optimum maturity, and freshness of the product. Even with high quality, fresh produce, it is imperative to freeze foods on the day when they are at their peak of maturity or ripeness for eating fresh.

- Freezing is a quick, convenient and easy way to preserve foods in the home. Plan ahead to manage your time and energy for preserving food directly from harvest. Freeze limited amounts at one time so the work is spread over several days of picking, rather than squeezed into one long tiring period of time. Be practical about what you attempt.

- A good rule for home freezing is two hours from garden or orchard to container, and the faster the better!

- A plus for home freezing is that slight variations in following directions do not result in a botulism hazard. The bacterium that causes botulism cannot grow in the freezer.

- Storage periods vary with each food but generally are about a year. If recommended storage periods are exceeded, taste may be affected, but as long as the product has been kept at 0°F or below, there is no question of safety. Be careful to use the oldest products first.

- Besides the initial cost of the freezer itself, energy costs are significant. Utilize the freezer fully to keep the energy costs per unit as low as possible. Fill the freezer when foods are least expensive.

- Some refrigerator-freezers are not designed for long-term storage. Keep a cold-temperature thermometer in your refrigerator-freezer and periodically check the temperature. It should be at 0°F (-20C) or colder. Free-standing freezers operate most efficiently when kept completely full. Package home-frozen foods in small quantities. The centers of large packages are slow to freeze and cause the freezer to run longer than necessary. Arrange containers throughout the freezer until they are frozen solid.

- **Remember if the electricity is off:** First—use perishable foods and foods from the refrigerator. Second—use foods from freezer (keep a list of freezer contents on outside, so you can cut down on opening it). Third—begin to use non-perishable food and staples.

- Check the plug itself for a firm fit. If the plug is loose in the receptacle, it may fall or be easily bumped out without notice. Replace loose plugs. Better yet, some hardware stores sell clips that clamp the plug in by means of the screw that holds the receptacle plate onto the outlet. Freezer owners should know where the closest commercial freezer is in case of an extensive failure. Check your home freezer after thunderstorms or power failures, since freezers have been known to be damaged occasionally when power fails or surges.

- **What to do when the freezer fails:** Don't panic when your freezer fails. Freezers are well insulated, and each package of frozen food acts as a block of ice protecting the food around it.

  Ordinarily, a fully stocked freezer will keep food frozen for two days after losing power. A half-full freezer can maintain freezing power for roughly one day.

  So, the first thing to find out is how long your freezer will be out. If it can be started again within a safe time, you don't need to do anything. Just resist the temptation to keep looking inside. Each time you open the door, warm air rushes in, reducing the freezer's effectiveness.

  However, if it can't be re-started in a day or two, you may want to:
  - Divide your food up among friends' freezers.
  - Find a store, church, or school freezer that will temporarily accept your food, or, if possible, rent space in a commercial freezer or cold storage plant.
  - Put dry ice in your freezer. Dry ice must be handled carefully. *Never touch it with your hands*. It freezes everything it touches.

  If possible, have the merchant put the dry ice in your picnic cooler or in a cardboard box. This makes handling it in the car easier.

  If you must remove it from the carrying case

when you get home, use heavy gloves or tongs. Work with dry ice in a well-ventilated area. As it evaporates, dry ice can quickly drive the oxygen you need to breathe out of a small area.

Place the dry ice on empty shelves in the freezer around the items to be kept frozen—not directly touching the packages themselves. You can also put a layer of cardboard over the freezer items and place the ice on top of the cardboard.

Twenty-five pounds of dry ice should hold a ten-cubic-foot full freezer below freezing for three-four days. If the freezer is half full, the same amount of ice will keep it stable for two-three days.

Judging your food *after* a freezer-thaw—Do not stick your head down into the freezer after it's been full of dry ice for several hours. There may not be enough oxygen left for you to breathe. Open the freezer and let outside air mix in before examining your food.

Meat or poultry that still contains ice crystals may safely be refrozen. For meat and poultry products that have been kept in a refrigerator section, though, or have only managed to stay cool, cooking is a better option. After you cook these items, you can refreeze them.

Throw out any product that has even a slightly unusual color or odor.

- **What to do when the refrigerator fails:** When power goes off in the refrigerator, you can normally expect your food to last at least four to six hours, depending on how warm your kitchen is. Higher room temperatures will mean it won't last as long.

  You can add block ice to the refrigerator to keep it cool if there's a delay in getting the power back on. Dry ice can be added to the freezer compartment.

- **FREEZING ACCESSORIES**

☐ You will need general kitchen utensils plus a steel, aluminum or enamel kettle large enough to hold at least one gallon of boiling water, with a tight fitting cover. Use a mesh basket, a strainer, or large squares of cheesecloth to hold one pound of vegetables in the boiling water.

- Steaming of cut, sliced or green leafy vegetables is recommended and will preserve more nutrients than water does.

☐ You will need a container to hold ice water for quick chilling of vegetables to stop cooking action. Drain thoroughly in a colander and turn out on absorbent towels.

- It is false economy to skimp on wrappings and containers. They should protect the food from cold air, which is dry, so as to retain the moisture in foods and prevent freeze burn and dehydration. Select them according to the use they will be put to.

☐ Most freezer containers on the market today are easy to seal, waterproof, and give satisfactory results. Rigid plastic containers, bags, and jars with wide tops are favorites.

☐ Moisture- and vapor-resistant wraps, which are exceptionally effective at excluding oxygen, include heavyweight aluminum foil, coated and laminated papers, polyethylene films, saran, and polyester films. They should be strong and pliable so the wrap will adhere readily to irregularly shaped objects, and eliminate as much air as possible to avoid frost accumulation inside. Careful wrapping is of no avail if the package breaks. It should be easily sealed, either by heatsealing or freezer tape.

☐ Freezer bags are available, and freeze-and-cook bags that withstand temperatures from below 0°F to above the boiling point. The freeze-and-cook bags are suitable for freezing and reheating food. Points to consider include the size convenient for your use and the cost.

DRYING

- **Preserving food by drying is the oldest method of food preservation, dating back to pre-biblical times.** Dried foods, either commercially dried or home dried, have a moisture content of 10-25 percent. Dried foods in a dry container in a cool, dark location will store approximately three years or as long as it smells and looks good. Suitable moisture-proof containers for dried fruits and vegetables include glass jars, tin cans with tightly fitting lids, and plastic containers. Containers should be filled as full as possible without crushing. The finished product should be labeled and dated.

- Drying is a comparatively simple process, requiring little outlay of equipment, time and money. It is economical, since it does not require sugar, jars and such materials used in other methods of preservation. Even though drying is not difficult, it does take time, constant attention, skill, and understanding of the principles of food drying methods. It can add variety to the diet.

- Food can be dried in the sun, in the oven, or in a dehydrator. Because dried foods are subjected to heat during the drying process, the nutritional value of dried foods is not as high as dehydrated or freeze-dried foods.

- Good drying fruits are apples, peaches, apricots, pears, plums, prunes, cherries, figs, grapes, and berries (except strawberries).

- A fruit treat that is expensive to buy in the stores can be made easily at home. It is fruit leather and is made by drying fruit pulp into a thin sheet and then rolling it up for storage. Sometimes called fruit rolls or fruit taffies, these "leathers" can be eaten as is, or they can be made into a beverage by adding five parts of water to one part leather in a food blender. They can also be used in pie filling, in cooking, and as a topping for dessert. Any type of fruit can be used: apricots, apples, grapes, berries, pineapples, oranges, pears, peaches, tomatoes, plums, tropical fruits, and others. Not usually suitable are grapefruits, lemons, persimmons, and rhubarb—without certain modifications.

- Low moisture foods have been dehydrated to remove 80-95 percent of the moisture. These include the dehydrated and freeze-dried foods. They store well and retain vitamin content better than many canned or dried foods.

- **Some have said that dehydrated foods will keep indefinitely. That is not true.** Dehydrated foods packaged in an inert gas atmosphere (nitrogen) and sealed in an airtight container will store for about 10-15 years. Thus, dehydrated foods should be rotated and consumed as part of the regular diet. Regular consumption of dehydrated foods will also help your family become accustomed to them. Also, don't forget to have additional water stored with dried foods in case water is not available.

- Freeze-dried foods are usually precooked, then flash-frozen, then dried slowly. The resulting product closely resembles the fresh product in size, shape and taste, but because the moisture has been removed, it is very lightweight and porous. Freeze drying makes possible the dependable and safe long-term storage of meats, fish, eggs, fruits and vegetables. Because it is usually precooked, freeze-dried foods usually need little or no cooking, needing only hot or cold water added for reconstituting. Freeze-dried food is available in meal-size pouches, as well as #10 and #2½ size cans.

- Vegetables dried to five percent residual moisture take longer to rehydrate than fruit dried to 20 percent residual moisture content.

- Small or thin pieces of fruits and vegetables rehydrate in less time than large pieces.

- Blanched vegetables rehydrate more quickly than unblanched vegetables.

- Boiling water shortens rehydration time.

- Rehydration is quicker in soft water than in hard water.

- Sugar and salt increase time for food rehydration; add at final five minutes for best results.

SMOKING AND CURING

- **Smoked meat has a very palatable flavor. Smoking is a simple process of "drying out" the meat.** Smoking tends to inhibit bacterial action. Cool smoked meats need no refrigeration. If electricity should go off for a long period of time, meats in frozen storage could be thawed and smoked. Most kinds of meat can be smoked—hams, fish, wild game (tougher cuts make good jerky—cut along the grain, not across it), beef, lamb, turkey, chicken, and fresh homemade sausage stuffed in narrow muslin bags. Types of smokers include: Small building, wooden barrel, box, old ice box, electric refrigerator, or a portable smoker from the sport shop that fits in the fireplace.

- **Use of large amounts of curing agents, such as nitrates and nitrites, may produce cancer-causing substances** and is limited by law in the United States.

On Saturday, June 5, 1976, at about 11:00 a.m., a warning of impending disaster was called to the Sheriff's Office in Rexburg, Idaho. Law enforcement agencies began at once to evacuate residents to higher ground. At 11:57 a.m., the Teton dam burst and a tremendous thirty-foot wall of water surged through the opening and thundered down the canyon, destroying nearly everything in its path. Seventeen miles of water was backed up behind the Teton Dam.

The water descended onto Sugar City, Idaho where it all but buried nearly every house and building in town. Most of them disappeared without a trace, except for the cement foundation.

The flood waters reached Rexburg, Idaho shortly after 2:00 p.m. As the waters coursed through the community, they picked up huge logs at the lumber mill, boats at a sporting goods store, and cars wherever they were parked. These became floating missiles of destruction as they ramrodded and mowed down buildings in their path.

By late afternoon, the flood waters had left Rexburg and Sugar City and were on their way down the Teton River to pour into the Snake River. Then on to Roberts, Idaho Falls, Firth and Blackfoot, leaving wreckage and ruin wherever they went.

Teton Dam near Rexburg, Idaho, June 1976. National Weather Service photo.

SALTING AND BRINING

- **Salting and brining is a simple, inexpensive method and requires no special equipment, materials or skill.** In many rural areas, or when it isn't feasible to freeze, dry or can, this method is used to preserve both meat and vegetables. And if the electricity supply were cut off for a considerable period, this method would be a good way to prevent the spoilage of food in the deep freeze.

Surging flood waters from the collapsed Teton Dam raged through a 100-mile stretch of the Teton and Snake Rivers, brought suffering and losses to nearly 5,000 families. Several thousand homes and businesses were destroyed or damaged.

About 7,800 people lived in the immediate path of the flood, and another 30,000 lived further down the valley. Residents had only minutes warning of the fast approaching wall of water. Experts say that there should have been about 5,300 people killed; however, only six people perished in the flood, in what was termed a miracle.

The Teton flood impressed many Saints with the need to have a portable emergency supply (72-hour kit) that's ready to be thrown into the car at a moment's notice.

Sugar City, Idaho, June 1976. American Red Cross photo.

FERMENTATION

- Preservation of food by controlling the acid content can be achieved in two ways. One is to naturally ferment the food—turning cabbage into sauerkraut. The other is to add an organic acid to the food to reduce the pH—adding vinegar to cucumbers to make pickles. Some foods such as berries and fruits naturally contain enough organic acids so their pH is below 4.6, and preservation of these foods requires only a boiling water bath heat treatment or freezing.

The partial or total collapse of structures is the main cause of earthquake deaths and injury. This was vividly demonstrated in the Mexico City earthquake where at least 10,000 people perished in hundreds of buildings that were not built to be earthquake resistant.
In this photo, rescue workers from the Mexican Red Cross hunt for survivors in the rubble of ruined buildings.
Mexico City earthquake, September 1985, American Red Cross photo.

PICKLING

Pickles or relishes can add zip and zest to your meals, snacks and party refreshments. They contain small amounts of nutrients, depending on ingredients used in making them. But they have little or no fat and are low in calories, except for the sweet varieties. Sun-drying, salting, smoking and pickling were methods used in ancient times for preserving food. Pickling is still popular today. Pickling is preserving foods in vinegar or brine or a combination of the two. Other ingredients are sometimes added to make pickles crisp and spicy.

"One of the worst of our disasters was down in the San Fernando valley. We were concerned when days went by and we couldn't get communication because the telephones were jammed, and there was no way of getting word as to how our people were faring; so we got in touch with our Regional Representative just outside of the earthquake area and asked if he could get us word. And the word came back, 'We are all right. We have drawn on the storage of foodstuffs that we have put aside. We had water stored.' The regular water was contaminated and people were distressed and in danger because of the contamination of the water; but the people who listened, had stored water as well as foodstuffs, and the other things to tide them through; and even though they didn't all have foodstuffs and didn't have water, those who listened and prepared didn't fear, and they set about together in a marvelous way to help each other...

"... So today, you folks who are the leaders of our stakes and wards, this is not a time for us to relax our vigilance. This is a time for us to, shall I say, reorganize our forces, build upon the experiences of the past, look to the future with confidence, because we are prepared, because we are going to need all the preparation that we have made when the times ahead of us shall be upon us. The Lord has so spoken and he expects us to do our part to prepare for these things that he has prophesied would shortly come to pass." (Harold B. Lee, Welfare Agricultural Meeting, April 1971.)

Collapsed overpass connecting Foothill Boulevard and Golden State Freeway. San Fernando earthquake (magnitude 6.5), Los Angeles County, California, 1971. Photo courtesy of U.S. Geological Survey.

- **Another option is "live storage."** In many circumstances where it is unlwawful to store food on shelves it is perfectly legal to store it **"on the hoof"** in the form of cows, chickens, goats, sheep, pigs, etc., or in a constantly used garden; and thus it is possible to maintain a considerable supply of some basic foods.

- Provision for adequate feed for the animals must be considered.

A hurricane is a cyclonic wind, moving at a speed of 74 miles per hour or more. Its center, or eye, with a diamter of from 7 to 20 miles, is a spiral of low pressure, a place of calm, where winds blow lazily and skies are clear. Around this core, the air moves at terrifying speeds of up to 200 miles an hour.

Heavy rains accompany the winds. The power of a hurricane is sobering. Taking in and converting to energy a quarter of a million tons of water every second, the average hurricane generates a force equal to 500,000 atom bombs. A recorded hurricane in Puerto Rico dumped 2½ billion tons of water in about three hours which was only a fraction of its total outpouring.

Photo courtesy of the National Oceanic and Atmospheric Administration, Miami, Florida, 1948.

NON-FOOD ITEMS

- **GENERAL:**
- [ ] Basic tools, including an axe, hatchet, pick and shovel.
- [ ] Wrench (to turn off gas in an emergency).
- [ ] Buckets (various sizes).
- [ ] Garbage bags (all sizes).
- [ ] Plastic bags (all sizes).
- [ ] Hangers.
- [ ] Wheat grinder.
- [ ] Seed and nut grinder.
- [ ] Extra brooms, mops.
- [ ] Rat and mouse traps, fly paper, roach strips.
- [ ] Rat poison.
- [ ] Burlap sacks.
- [ ] Wooden crates, storage boxes.
- [ ] Transistor radios, alkaline batteries.
- [ ] Flashlights, alkaline batteries.
- [ ] Extra batteries (for other home uses).
- [ ] Fire-fighting supplies such as buckets, sand, water, hoses, ladder, fire extinguishers, smoke detectors.
- [ ] Pencils, paper.
- [ ] Office supplies.
- [ ] Electrical basics.
- [ ] Fuses.
- [ ] Light bulbs.
- [ ] Extra furnace filters, swamp cooler pads.
- [ ] Push-type, non-electric carpet cleaner.
- [ ] Large metal garbage cans (many uses).
- [ ] Hot water bottle, ice bag.
- [ ] Dog leash. (When food is scarce, a leash will help protect your dog and other people.)
- [ ] Work gloves (several pairs).
- [ ] Camera film. Keep cool and dry.
- [ ] Dosimeter (fallout radiation meter).
- [ ] Wind-up alarm clocks.

- [ ] Life jacket for each family member.
- [ ] Hand pump or plastic siphon.
- [ ] Standard ammunition.

- **REPAIR MATERIALS:**
- [ ] Heavy wire, rope and twine.
- [ ] Heavy plastic sheeting.
- [ ] Extra lumber of all sizes.
- [ ] Nails, screws, bolts, etc.
- [ ] Non-electric drills, hand saws, etc.
- [ ] Various tapes—duct, masking, Scotch, electrical.
- [ ] Plumbing repair materials, such as faucet washers, drain openers, etc.
- [ ] Caulking gun and caulking.
- [ ] Rubber patch kit for repairing bicycle tires, etc.
- [ ] Various glues.

- **AUTOMOBILE NEEDS:**
- [ ] Oil, grease, grease gun.
- [ ] Oil filters.
- [ ] Spare tires.
- [ ] Power steering, transmission, and brake fluid.
- [ ] Battery booster cables.
- [ ] Spare belts for every belt used in engine.
- [ ] Spare hoses and clamps.
- [ ] Tire sealant inflater (pressurized can).
- [ ] Liquid radiator sealant.
- [ ] Ice scrapers, brushes, windshield wiper fluid.
- [ ] Hand operated tire inflater.
- [ ] Tool kit.
- [ ] Automobile winter "storm" kit.
- [ ] ABC-type fire extinguisher.
- [ ] Emergency road distress flares.
- [ ] Extra pair of windshield wiper blades.
- [ ] Plastic siphon pump.
- [ ] Air filters.

☐ Extra spark plugs, points.

• Alternate transportation (fuel efficient).

☐ Bicycle for each family member.

☐ Mo-peds (150 miles to the gallon).

☐ Snowmobiles.

☐ Four-wheelers.

☐ Family horse.

☐ Spare fuel and parts for the above and extra feed for the horse.

Practical things a family can do in the home to help prevent damage and injury from an earthquake include:

(1) Stabilize water heater with metal straps to wall studs; (2) Use flexible connectors where gas lines meet appliances; (3) Keep fire extinguisher in accessible place; (4) Locate main electrical and gas switches for emergency shut-off; (5) Keep all breakables in low or secure cabinets; (6) Replace heavy hangings over bed with lightweight alternatives; (7) Place secure latches on cupboards to prevent doors from swinging open; (8) Secure top-heavy furniture to wall studs with metal braces; (9) Keep 72-hour emergency kits on hand; (10) Earthquake-proof food storage by locating heavy and breakable storage items on or near the floor, padding individual jars with newspapers or foam, and by installing a strip of wood on the fronts of shelves to prevent shelf contents from falling off.

This house was damaged by displacement along a fault during the San Fernando earthquake on February 9, 1971 (magnitude 6.5). The house has been shortened and racked by compressional movement across the break. The garage, on the left side of the fault, has been carried toward the opposite end of the house, built on the right side of the fault break.

Photo courtesy of U.S. Geological Survey.

GARDEN SEEDS AND EQUIPMENT

☐ **Store a year's supply of garden vegetable seeds.** Buy this year's and next year's at the same time. Seeds should be stored in tightly sealed jars and kept in a cool, dark, dry storage areas.

• You will seldom plant all the seeds in a package in one year. You can save seeds, but not all of them will last the same length of time, even those in unopened packages. As a general rule, vegetable seeds should not be stored for longer than five years, although cool, dry storage will extend this lifetime.

• Approximate storage time for vegetable seeds:

> 1 year—sweet corn, onion, parsley, parsnip.
> 2 years—beet, pepper.
> 3 years—asparagus, bean, celery, carrot, lettuce, pea, spinach, tomato.
> 4 years—cabbage, cauliflower, eggplant, okra, pumpkin, radish, squash.
> 5 years—cucumber, endive, muskmelon, watermelon.

• A free vegetable seed catalog may be obtained by writing to either W. Atlee Burpee Co., Box 748, Riverside, Ca 99504 or Gurney Seed & Nursery Co., 1448 Page Street, Yankton, South Dakota 57078.

• Very few tools are necessary for a small garden. It is better to buy a few simple, high-grade tools that will serve well for many years than equipment that is poorly designed or made of cheap or low-grade meterials that will not last. Following is a list of tools, materials, and equipment you may wish to acquire and have on hand as part of your gardening program.

☐ Greenhouse or cold frame—A greenhouse is a specialized structure designed for growing plants year-round. A clear or translucent cover permits sunlight to enter, which heats the greenhouse during the day. When excessive sun heating occurs, ventilation is needed. During cold nights and much of cold days, a heating system is required to maintain the desired temperature.

☐ **Extra bags of chemical garden fertilizers.**

☐ Bags of sterile steer manure or other soil conditioner. Leaves and grass clippings work fine.

☐ Extra bags of lawn fertilizer and extra lawn sprinklers, and hoses.

☐ Wheel-type hand fertilizer distributor.

☐ Push type hand lawnmower.

☐ Materials to construct a compost pile (lumber and mesh wire).

☐ A wide variety of vegetable garden and fruit and nut tree pesticides and necessary application equipment. Check with your local agricultural extension agent, garden center, or an experienced gardener for advice and recommendations about which pesticides to store for your area. (Storage life is at least two years.)

☐ Garden spade or shovel.

☐ Garden hoe—pointed and straight.

☐ Single-wheel hoe (used for most work usually done with a common hoe but with much less effort).

☐ Steel bow garden rake.

☐ Garden hand trowel.

☐ Weeder.

☐ Digging fork to extract weeds.

☐ Stakes and cord or twine for laying out rows.

☐ Pitchfork.

☐ Rotary garden tiller and extra fuel. (Useful in preparing the soil for planting and controlling weeds; however, they are fairly expensive.)

☐ Seeding tools, such as a hand seeder, vibrator seeder, or push planter.

☐ Wheelbarrow.

☐ Linseed oil to keep wooden garden tool handles in good shape.

☐ Pruning shears.

☐ File to keep garden tools sharp.

☐ Several coils of galvanized bailing wire (many garden uses).

☐ Water diffuser to keep water from making holes in the garden when a large stream is used.

☐ Extra one or two lengths of garden hose for watering, siphoning, and for emergency firefighting. Make sure your garden hose is long enough to stretch throughout your home.

☐ Poles for staking tomatoes and beans.

- [ ] Six-inch mesh concrete reinforcing wire is best to support tomato plants by forming a circle 18 inches in diameter around the plant and attaching to a wood stake, driven in the ground.
- [ ] Plastic sheeting (heavy duty) for mulching and fashioning a makeshift greenhouse or cold frame.
- [ ] Bushel baskets.
- [ ] Burlap sacks for potatoes, root crops.
- [ ] Mesh onion bags.
- [ ] Several buckets.
- [ ] Hotcaps. (One gallon plastic milk jugs with the bottom cut out work well for this purpose.)
- [ ] Seed starter and transplant containers (to start seedlings indoors or in a greenhouse), such as cans, peat pots, clay pots, soil pellets, milk cartons, egg cartons, or buckets.

- [ ] Indoor sterile potting soil.
- You may want to have a sample of your garden soil tested to determine which fertilizers and soil conditioners need to be added to your soil to produce optimally. (Check with your local extension agent as to where to send your soil sample for analysis. There is a fee for this service.)
- [ ] Books and instruction manuals on vegetable gardening and growing fruit and nut trees, berry bushes, etc.
- For a nominal fee, you can obtain the booklet, *Getting Along with Your Garden*, by writing to: Ezra Taft Benson Institute, Brigham Young University, Provo, Utah 84602.

The State Capitol building looms in the background over floodwaters as they flow out of City Creek Canyon on to State Street in downtown Salt Lake City. It is interesting to note that Salt Lake City is an arid, semi-desert city, Utah being one of the driest states in the nation. Salt Lake City, Utah, May 1983.

CLOTHING AND BEDDING

- **A year's supply should include sufficient durable clothing and bedding to accommodate your family's needs for at least a year.** Do not try to meet all clothing needs in storing, only the basics, but base your choices on ages of family members, your climate and seasons. Give some thought to storing clothing that can be worn by either boys or girls. Stick to classic, simple styles and classic colors and patterns. Include clothes that are not readily outdated, clothes that can be mixed or matched, dressed up or down. Also, keep clean, used clothing on hand to remodel, cut down for younger family members, or refurbish, if needed.

- Special emphasis should be given to winter clothing items such as:

- ☐ A warm winter coat (wool).

- The warmest and all around best winter coat or parka is comprised of a GOR-TEX outer shell, with either goose down insulation or a synthetic insulation such as quallofil.

- ☐ Raingear

- ☐ Wool socks

- ☐ Extra shoes, snow moonboots, or rubber boots

- ☐ Thermal underwear

- ☐ Mittens (warmer than fingered gloves). Old socks work fine.

- ☐ Several pairs of warm, multi-purpose gloves

- ☐ A warm hat or ski-type cap

- Wool clothing repels water and has the unique property of keeping the body warm even if it gets wet.

- Wool is a natural thermostatic insulator that keeps you warm in the winter and cool in the summer. Wool is naturally durable and can withstand rugged and tough wear.

- Good inexpensive clothing can be found at thrift stores, rummage and garage sales, factory outlets, or one can shop large department store holiday sales for bargains.

- Keep a list of family clothing needs and sizes with you to take advantage of good buys.

- Develop home sewing skills necessary to supply personal and family sewing needs.

- Store only clean clothing and fabrics in a dark, dry, cool, bug and dust-free environment if possible. Hanging clothing must be covered or stored in suit-type boxes. Otherwise, storage may be in clean, large plastic trash cans with lids, bins, boxes, suit-cases, zippered garment bags, footlockers, chests of drawers, or cedar chests.

Basic sewing and mending supplies include:

- ☐ Scissors and shears
- ☐ Needles in assorted sizes
- ☐ Sewing machine needles
- ☐ Upholstering needles
- ☐ Pins and pin cushion
- ☐ Safety pins
- ☐ Patterns
- ☐ Seam ripper
- ☐ Masking tape
- ☐ Crochet hooks and knitting needles
- ☐ Thread in assorted sizes and colors used most often
- ☐ Laces and trims
- ☐ Notions (snaps, zippers, hooks and eyes, etc.)
- ☐ Chalk
- ☐ Elastic
- ☐ Pellon
- ☐ Buttons
- ☐ Thimbles
- ☐ Sewing machine bobbins
- ☐ Shoelaces (various sizes and colors)
- ☐ Shoe polish
- ☐ Extra shoe soles and inner soles
- ☐ Shoe repair kit
- ☐ Yardstick
- ☐ Tape measure
- ☐ Iron
- ☐ Bonding fabrics
- ☐ Seam and hem tapes or binding

- [ ] Sewing and mending manual
- [ ] Sewing machine oil and brush
- [ ] Six-inch seam gauge
- [ ] Tracing wheel and carbon
- [ ] Darning spool (or use a light bulb)
- [ ] Press cloth
- [ ] Glue (for fabric and shoe mending)
- [ ] Clothesline and pins
- [ ] A good sewing machine which can be converted to work manually or with a treadle in case of extended power outages.
- [ ] Yarn (wool or acrylic in assorted colors)
- **Store a good supply of classic, multi-purpose fabrics such as:**
- [ ] Cotton (flannel and muslin)
- Each year, Americans use over four billion pounds of cotton or over 20 pounds per person.
- [ ] Linen
- [ ] Wool
- [ ] Silk
- [ ] Corduroy
- [ ] Denim
- [ ] Perma press
- Firmly woven fabrics wear longer than lightweight fabrics.
- Dark-colored clothing (prints and plaids) will look nice longer, not showing the soil and wear as quickly as light-colored and solid-colored clothes.
- [ ] Diamond point needles and unwaxed dental floss for sewing and repairing leather items
- [ ] Stain remover
- [ ] Spray-on stain repellent
- [ ] Spray-on water repellent
- [ ] Extra hangers
- [ ] Mothproofing insecticide (in liquid, spray, crystal, or flake form)

- [ ] Store an extra pair of shoes and boots that are new or in good repair
- [ ] Leatherworking tools and equipment
- [ ] Cheesecloth (lots of uses)
- Basic clothing storage for infants includes lots of cloth diapers (six dozen), undershirts, sleepers, sweater, cap, jacket, pants, dress up outfits, waterproof pants, booties, flannel receiving blankets, and heavy wrapping blankets or sleeping bag.
- [ ] Bath towels, hand towels, dish towels
- [ ] Dishcloths, washcloths, and tablecloths.
- Basic bedding items to store include:
- [ ] Sleeping bags
- The warmest fills (insulation) in sleeping bags are about three pounds of goose down or synthetic quallofil, hollofil 808, hollofil 2, or polarguard.
- [ ] Emergency blanket (50 inches wide by 82 inches long, 12 ounces, waterproof and windproof, mylar material evolved from insulation used in space exploration reflects back 90 percent of body heat)
- [ ] Quilts (lots of heavy ones)
- Old material scraps, old clothing, sheets or drapes can be fashioned into a quilt
- Newspaper pages sandwiched between blankets on a bed and under the sheet provide amazing insulation if you have nothing better.
- [ ] Several large blankets (wool is the warmest)
- [ ] Several baby blankets
- Baby blankets can be sewn together to fashion a large blanket or quilt
- [ ] Several extra bedsheets for each bed and crib
- Bandages or quilt tops can be made from old bedsheets
- Save cotton flour and sugar bags to fashion into clothing, quilts, or pillows
- [ ] Extra quilt batts
- Store quilts and sheets in large plastic trashbags to keep them clean and dry
- [ ] Extra pillows

Bitter cold and winter storms can cause extremely serious hazards for the homebound as well as for those who must be outside. Since winter transportation becomes more difficult, keep your car in top operating condition and the gas tank as nearly full as possible. Also, it is wise to carry a "winter storm car kit" for safer winter travel.

If isolated at home after a winter storm or major disaster, a prepared family may draw upon their year's supply of stored food and water, extra clothing, bedding, and reserve fuel.

With the possibility of power failures, freezing or broken pipes, and other problems, the provident and self-reliant family will have made provision for emergency heating and lighting, as well as sanitation.

Adams, New York, 1977. Photo courtesy of the National Oceanic and Atmospheric Administration.

TOILETRIES AND SANITATION

- **In a disaster situation, plumbing may not be usable as a result of disrupted water and sewer lines due to flooding, freezing, an earthquake, or a number of other circumstances.** Thus it is necessary to sanitize human waste in a manner to avoid infection and spread of disease.

- If lines are broken, but the toilet itself is usable, the bowl can be lined with a plastic bag. If it is unusable, a plastic bag in a bucket may be substituted.

- **Four types of disinfectant may be used. Choose one to store with your one-year supply.**

- ☐ If water is available, a solution of one part liquid chlorine bleach to ten parts water is best. (Don't use dry bleach, which is caustic and not safe for this type of use.)

- ☐ HTH, or calcium hypochlorite, is available at swimming pool supply stores. HTH is intended to be used in solution. Following directions, it can be mixed and stored.

- ☐ Portable toilet chemicals, both liquid and dry, are available at recreational vehicle (RV) supply stores. These chemicals are designed especially for toilets which are not connected to sewer lines. Use according to package directions.

- ☐ Powdered, chlorinated lime is available at building supply stores. It can be used dry. Be sure to get chlorinated lime, not quick lime, which is highly alkaline and corrosive.

- **CAUTION—Chlorinated products which are intended to be mixed with water for use can be dangerous if used dry.**

- ☐ Several five-gallon plastic polyethylene buckets with tight-fitting lids or five-gallon metal containers with tight-fitting lids should be stored as makeshift toilets. A seat can be fashioned from a hole cut in the seat of an old chair, or a toilet seat can be purchased to place on the bucket.

- Porta-potties are available on the market (more comfortable than a bucket).

- ☐ One or more large metal covered garbage cans should be available to contain wastes.

- ☐ A good supply of plastic liners (5-6 gallon size) and twist-ties should be stored.

- **Store also a year's supply of the following:**

☐ Large lawn and leaf size trash bags (many uses).

☐ Large grocery sacks and grocery cellophane bags (for use in conjunction with disposal of solid wastes).

☐ Save all newspapers possible for use in waste disposal, as well as fuel, and many other emergency uses.

☐ A good shovel

☐ Lysol-type disinfectant

☐ Deodorizer tablets and air fresheners

☐ Ammonia

☐ Laundry detergent, one that can be used in cold water as well as hot.

☐ Liquid bleach for washing and to purify water.

☐ Stain remover sprays

☐ Fabric softeners

☐ A couple of washtubs, a hand-operated wringer (**available at auto supply stores**), and a plumber's friend (used as an agitator) may prove useful for washing clothes if there is no electricity for an extended period of time.

☐ Clothesline and clothespins

☐ Paper towels

☐ Scrubbing sponges or scouring pads

☐ Waterproof gloves

☐ Clean rags

☐ Cleanser

☐ Dish detergent

☐ Laundry detergent

☐ Bar soap (save soap scraps and press together into a new bar).

☐ Shampoo and conditioner

☐ Toothpaste and toothbrushes

☐ Pre-moistened towelettes

☐ Deodorant, hair spray

☐ Denture cream and cleanser

☐ Toilet tissue, facial tissue

- [ ] Feminine supplies
- [ ] Infant supplies, such as diaper ointment, baby powder, baby lotion.
- [ ] Special nursing needs (pads, etc.)
- [ ] A plastic sink with a hand pump which holds five gallons of water inside is an item you may wish to have on hand.
- [ ] Insect repellent
- [ ] Shaving supplies
- [ ] Extra pair of eyeglasses, contact lens, and lens cleaning solutions.
- [ ] Five-gallon solar shower (a bag of water heated by the sun).
- A makeshift bathtub can also be made by digging a trench in the ground, lining it with insulative newspapers and thick plastic sheeting, then filling it with water heated by the fireplace.
- [ ] A manual carpet sweeper may be useful if your electric vacuum cleaner is not functional because of no power.
- [ ] Extra broom and mopheads

- Knowing the location of the nearest natural hot springs may be helpful if heated water is hard to come by.
- A spray bottle can be used as a makeshift shower, especially for small children.
- [ ] Rubbing alcohol
- [ ] Vaseline
- [ ] Mineral oil
- [ ] Lye (used in soap making)
- A booklet entitled *Housecleaning on a Shoestring* is available by writing to the Cooperative Extension Service, Utah State University, Logan, Utah 84321. It contains useful recipes to make homecleaning products out of basic ingredients found in the home.
- Basic cleaning ingredients to store for the recipes include:
- [ ] Ammonia, vinegar, baking soda, washing soda, whiting, mineral spirits, boiled linseed oil, soap jelly, liquid detergent, rubbing alcohol, pine oil, gum turpentine, and kerosene. (Look for these items at supermarkets and paint, hardware or drugstores.)

"I am profoundly grateful for the essence of that spirit of helpfulness which has come down through the generations and which has been so evident in the troubles Latter-day Saints experience in time of disaster or difficulty. The mayor of Salt Lake City told me that when the Salt Lake City flood situation became serious one Sunday afternoon in 1983 that he called a Stake President. Within a very short time 4,000 volunteers showed up. The story of such mutual helpfulness caught the attention of many individuals and publications across the nation. Latter-day Saints, working together with their neighbors of other faiths, have labored with one another in times of distress and have been heralded on radio and television, in newspapers and magazines. Writers have treated it as if it were a new and unique phenomenon." (Gordon B. Hinkley, Ensign, July 1984.)

"This has been the only flood or natural disaster I've ever covered that was almost upbeat. There's no such thing as a good disaster story, but there were things about this disaster that were good, mostly the people!" (Barry Petersen, CBS News Correspondent, Salt Lake City, Utah, May 1983.)

Looking north on State Street in Salt Lake City one sees the State capitol, as volunteers work to build up and reinforce dikes in hopes of containing surging floodwaters flowing out of City Creek Canyon.

- **It is most important to work on updating your first aid skills. The life or death of a family member may depend on your first aid abilities.** The American Red Cross offers classes in first aid and CPR which cost little or nothing. It's wise to take advantage of these classes. You can upgrade your first aid kit according to the training you have in first aid. Include only items in your first aid kit you are familiar with and know how to use properly.

- **All family members should know the basics: how to open the airway, mouth to mouth, CPR, how to stop severe bleeding, and how to treat choking.**

- The basic objective is to rescue people whose lives are threatened, check for injuries and to provide emergency first aid if necessary.

- Remember that medical facilities may be overloaded after a severe disaster or crisis. Professional medical care may be unavailable for a long time.

- Each family member should be **adequately immunized** and up to date on booster shots.

- Each individual or family should carry **adequate health and life insurance**.

- Remember items for persons with special needs, such as diabetics, invalids, the handicapped, the elderly, infants, those with chronic illnesses, etc.

- **IMPORTANT NOTE: Life support systems should have an alternative power source readily available and in quantity to withstand the absence of electricity for an extended period of time.**

- Remember: You always have your most valuable equipment with you—the use of your hands and the breath of life in your lungs.

- **First aid items:**

- ☐ **Consecrated oil**

- ☐ Sterile dressings (gauze) in sealed paper packages: Sizes 2x2 inches, 4x4 inches, 6x6 inches. For dressing cuts, burns, and lacerations.

- ☐ Telfa non-sticking sterile pads 4"x4": Does not stick to the wound when bandaged.

- ☐ Post-op sponges, 4"x4": To control bleeding.

- ☐ Ace bandages, 2 and 3 inch widths: To hold dressings in place.

- ☐ Kerlix gauze rolls: To cover wounds.

- ☐ Conforming gauze bandages: For bandaging wounds.

- ☐ Sterile oval eye pads: To cover injured eyes.

- ☐ Muslin triangular bandages with safety pin: For use as a bandage, tourniquet, or arm sling.

- ☐ Vaseline gauze dressing, sterile: For chest wounds.

- ☐ Maternity or "OB" pads: To stop serious bleeding.

- ☐ Band-Aids, various sizes: For minor wounds.

- Bandages can be made from a white undershirt, handkerchiefs, or other cotton clothing in an emergency where ready-made materials are not available.

- ☐ Transpore surgical tape (best type): To hold bandages, dressings, and splints in place.

- ☐ Bandage-type scissors: For cutting bandages, gauze, tape, etc.

- ☐ Tourniquet, rubber or Velcro, 1" wide: To stop very severe bleeding.

- ☐ Large extrication (cervical) collar: Foam with Velcro type, to help immobilize a possibly fractured neck.

- ☐ Medium extrication (cervical) collar

- ☐ Small extrication (cervical) collar

- ☐ Assorted sizes of splints: To immobilize bone fractures.

- ☐ Wire or "ladder" type splints: For splinting broken bones.

- ☐ Sterile tongue blades: To check for sore throat and to splint broken fingers.

- Splints can also be fashioned from pillows, boards, ski poles, umbrellas, or rolled up newspapers. They can be secured with belts.

- Crutches can be fashioned from forked sticks if nothing better is available.

- ☐ Instant chemical disposable hotpack: Increases blood circulation, helps reduce pain.

- ☐ Instant chemical disposable coldpack: To reduce swelling, for burns, for relief of pain.

- ☐ Rubber hot water bottle: For relief of pain.

- ☐ Plastic ice bag: To reduce swelling, for burns, for relief of pain.

- [ ] "OB" kit: To assist in emergency childbirth.

- [ ] Sterile bulb aspirator, 2 or 3 ounce size: To extract blood and other secretions from the back of the throat and from the nostrils; essential for emergency childbirth.

- [ ] Laerdal-type pocket mask: As an aid to give mouth-to-mouth without actual contact to skin.

- [ ] Hudson-type airways, assorted sizes: To help keep the airway open.

- [ ] Mouth-to-mouth instructions: On a small card.

- [ ] Choking first aid instructions: On a small card.

- [ ] CPR instructions: On a small card.

- [ ] Rubbing alcohol (70%) isopropyl: For poison ivy, to sterilize, to cool the body (except infants), or to clean hands.

- [ ] Sterile water or normal saline solution in plastic bottle: For wound irrigation, cleansing, cooling burns.

- [ ] Small container or sterile liquid soap: For cleaning wounds, such as Phisoderm.

- [ ] Pair of latex sterile gloves: To prevent further contamination of wounds, reducing chances of infection.

- [ ] Oral thermometer, pencil case: To determine body temperature.

- [ ] Rectal thermometer, pencil case: To determine body temperature.

- [ ] Vaseline: For lubrication of rectal thermometer, for chapped lips, etc.

- [ ] Safety pins of various sizes: To tie bandages.

- [ ] Paper drinking cups: To give drinks and to cover eye injuries.

- [ ] One-ounce plastic measuring cup: For measuring out medicines.

- [ ] Syringe-type medication dispenser: 5cc's equals one teaspoon.

- [ ] First aid manual, American Medical Association: For first aid instructions.

- [ ] Reader's Digest First Aid Manual: For first aid instructions.

- [ ] Names, phone numbers, and addresses of physician, hospital, paramedics, police, fire department, poison control center, etc.

- [ ] Critical medical histories required by family members.

- [ ] Paper and pencil: To record medical information and to send messages.

- [ ] Small flashlight or reusable penlight with extra alkaline batteries: To examine throat and contractility of pupils of eyes and to offer medical assistance in dark situations.

- [ ] Emergency blanket 84"x56": To treat shock.

- [ ] Matches, waterproofed: To sterilize needles, scissors, or dressings.

- [ ] Emesis basin or "airsick bag": From commercial airlines or regular plastic bag and tie (for vomiting and hyperventilation).

- [ ] Cutter brand snake bite kit: For treatment of snake bites.

- [ ] Medic-Alert tags, bracelets or I.D. (if applicable).

- [ ] Q-tip cotton applicators: For application of skin medications.

- [ ] Extra contact lens

- [ ] Extra eyeglasses

- [ ] Extra hearing aid batteries

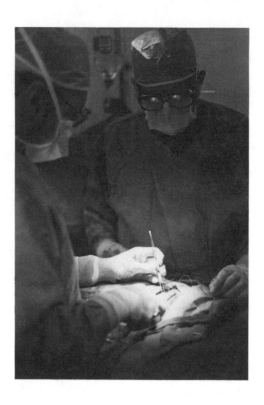

Since hospitals and emergency medical services may be overloaded following a major disaster, it is wise for all family members to gain a working knowledge of basic first aid and rescue skills. Quite often, life or death is usually in the hands of the nearest person, which in the home would mean responsible members of the family or the next door neighbor.

Family emergency preparedness plans should also include assembling a well-stock first-aid kit and at least a year's supply of essential medications required by family members. It is also critical to carry adequate health and life insurance and to get current with necessary immunizations and booster shots.

MEDICATIONS

- **Critical medications often become a very rare commodity during and after many disasters and other emergencies.** A needed medication will not only provide relief of physical discomfort and pain associated with injury or disease, but will, as a result, help reduce the level of stress and anxiety. It is wise to **work with and consult your physician and your local pharmacy in obtaining necessary medications for your year's supply.** Most medications should be rotated every year and should be stored in a cool, dry, dark location.

- Medicines for **chronic illnesses** usually require **daily medications.** Store a year's supply or more of these medications (diabetes, heart condition, etc.).

- Be sure all medicine containers are **adequately labeled** and that **directions for use** are kept with each of them.

- Keep a record of expiration dates of the medicine (usually located on the medicine label). Most medications can be used longer than the printed expiration date. Check with your doctor and pharmacist.

You may want to include the following medications:

- ☐ Adult aspirin tablets (analgesic)
- ☐ Adult Tylenol, Acetaminophen (analgesic)
- ☐ Strong pain medication for adults and children (prescription, consult your physician).
- ☐ Children's Tylenol, Acetaminophen (analgesic)
- ☐ Infant Tylenol drops, Acetaminophen (analgesic)
- ☐ Lomotil tablets or equivalent (prescription) for diarrhea.
- ☐ Paragoric liquid or equivalent (prescription) for relief of diarrhea.
- ☐ Pepto-Bismol or equivalent for relief of diarrhea. It is also an antacid.
- ☐ Antihistamine to dry nasal secretions.
- ☐ Decongestants to help clear stuffed nasal passages.
- ☐ Cough medicines to suppress an irritating cough. (One containing codeine also may be desirable for severe coughs.)
- ☐ Expectorants to help expel congested chest fluids.
- ☐ Laxative for relief of constipation.

- ☐ **Broad-spectrum antibiotics** have a wide range of coverage against bacteria. Though fairly expensive, ask your doctor for a supply of broad-spectrum antibiotics in powder form in both adult and children strengths. **Used in consultation with your physicians, this is perhaps one of the most critical items you can store in your year's supply.**

- ☐ Benadryl (Diphenhydramine) or equivalent for congestion, allergic reactions, itching or restlessness.

- ☐ **Potassium iodide tablets (at least 14 tablets for each family member) for prophylactic protection of the thyroid gland against radioactive iodine in the event of a nuclear incident. (The recent nuclear power plant meltdown in the Soviet Union placed an extremely heavy demand on potassium iodide tablets throughout many parts of the world.)**

- ☐ Calamine lotion for treatment of poison ivy, poison sumac, poison oak, and to soothe minor bites and stings.

- ☐ Syrup of Ipecac to induce vomiting in poison cases. **WARNING: Ipecac, distributed by HUMCO, may contain eucalyptus oil that can be fatal if ingested in quantities as small as one teaspoonful. Also, Ipecac, distributed by BRITE-LIFE, may contain harmful iodine. Both are extremely dangerous, and if found in your emergency supplies, you should contact authorities immediately.**

- ☐ Insect repellent: Roll-on, spray, or wipe on

- Crushed ferns or wild onions can be rubbed on as an insect repellent in an emergency if nothing else is available.

- ☐ Campho-phenique for minor wounds and insect bites.

- ☐ Cornstarch powder to treat diaper rash, if applicable.

- ☐ Desiten diaper ointment to treat diaper rash, if applicable.

- ☐ Neosporin ointment or equivalent for skin infections, antibacterial ointment for minor wounds.

- ☐ Alcohol preparation pads: Germacide to clean or disinfect a wound.

- ☐ Betadine preparation pads: Antiseptic, germacide, to clean or disinfect a wound.

- [ ] Hydrogen peroxide: Antiseptic for minor cuts and abrasions. Helps dissolve blood in clothing, etc.

- [ ] Block-out or pre-sun, paba-film, pabonol: For use as a sunscreen.

- [ ] Solarcaine or equivalent for sunburns.

- [ ] Chapstick for chapped lips.

- [ ] Hydrocortisone cream for itching skin.

- [ ] Vaseline Intensive Care Lotion for dry skin.

- [ ] Auralgan ear drops or equivalent (prescription) for ear infections.

- [ ] Antibiotic eye drops for eye infections (prescription). Consult your physician.

- [ ] Vaso-Clear eye drops or equivalent for eye irritations.

- [ ] Oil of cloves to place on cotton for toothaches.

- [ ] Compazine or equivalent (prescription) for nausea or vomiting.

- [ ] Morning sickness pills (prescription). Consult your physician to obtain a safe drug.

- [ ] Table salt to dilute with water to administer for delayed treatment of shock and burns and for treatment of heat cramps and fatigue and to make salt water to gargle with to treat a sore throat.

- [ ] Salt tablets for treatment of heat emergencies and fatigue.

- [ ] Baking soda in small container for third degree burns and shock.

- [ ] Sugar cubes individually wrapped in plastic or restaurant sugar packets for insulin shock.

- [ ] Oxygen, small canister and mask to treat shock and chronic lung diseases.

- Those using oxygen on an ongoing basis should make provision for a year's supply of it. Consult with your physician.

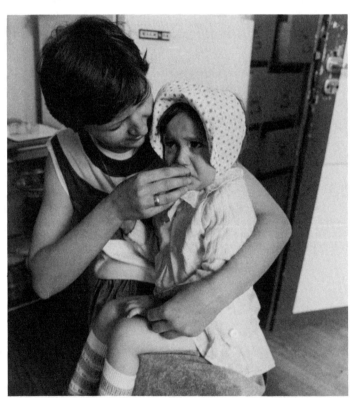

A young girl in this northern Polish town cries as she drinks a bitter potassium iodine solution to help combat the effects of radioactivity leaked from the Chernobyl power station in neighboring Soviet Union.

The April 26, 1986 explosion and fire at Russia's Chernobyl nuclear reactor sent radiation-laden clouds encircling much of the globe, bringing untold death and suffering.

Throughout the following weeks, an anxious, puzzled and increasingly frustrated world struggled to understand the extent of the disaster. The fallout caused an international uproar against the Soviet Union for its lax safety measures and its concealment of the fact that the dangerous radiation was floating toward neighboring countries.

The United States presently has over 100 similar reactors in use, each posing the potential for massive devastation.

Reuters/Bettman newsphotos, New York. Photo May 1, 1986, Bialystok, Poland.

INFANT NEEDS

- [ ] Disposable diapers—Figure 8 to 12 diapers a day for at least a year in small, medium, and large sizes.

- [ ] Cloth diapers—Six or more dozen. If you combine with disposables, you'll need about half this amount.

- [ ] Rubber pants (several pairs)

- [ ] Disposable diaper liners

- [ ] Safety pins for cloth diapers

- [ ] Moistened towelettes

- [ ] Diaper ointment, cornstarch, petroleum jelly

- [ ] Baby lotion, powder, oil, shampoo and soap

- [ ] **Liquid Acetaminophen** (Tylenol Exlixor and drops)

- [ ] **Tylenol with codeine** for severe pain such as ear infections. (Prescription. Consult your pediatrician for an extra bottle for storage. Rotate every three years.)

- [ ] **Cough medicine**—A cough medicine containing codeine may also be desirable to have on hand. Consult your pediatrician.

- [ ] **Decongestant medicine**

- [ ] **Antihistamine medicine**

- [ ] **Expectorant medicine**

- [ ] **Ear drops** for ear infections. (Prescription. Consult your pediatrician.)

- [ ] **Eye drops** for eye infections. (Prescription. Consult your pediatrician.)

- [ ] **Medicine for diarrhea and constipation.** Consult your pediatrician.

- [ ] **Colic medicine.** Consult your pediatrician.

- [ ] **Liquid vitamins, minerals, and fluoride supplements.** Consult your doctor.

- [ ] **Broad-spectrum antibiotics** in powder form. **Antibiotics can be life-saving** but must be used properly. Broad-spectrum antibiotics are effective against a wide variety of common "bugs" or infections. **Ask your pediatrician if he will prescribe several bottles for storage.** Stored in a cool, dark, dry and **childproof** location, unopened medicine including antibiotics may remain effective at least three years. **Ask your doctor for recommendations on each medicine.**

- [ ] Infant formula in liquid and powder. Shelf-life is no more than about three to four years under ideal storage conditions.

- [ ] Strained baby foods—Bottles. Shelf-life is about three to four years.

- [ ] Dried baby food mixes such as cereals. Shelf-life is about five years if repacked in airtight containers and stored in a cool, dry, dark location.

- [ ] Strained baby fruit juices in bottles or cans. Shelf-life is about two to three years under ideal storage conditions.

- [ ] Finger foods, such as graham crackers. Storage life is about one year if repacked in a metal, airtight container and stored under ideal storage conditions.

- [ ] Non-electric baby food mill, strainer

- [ ] Plastic baby bottles, nipples, sterilizer kit, scrub brushes, etc.

- [ ] Presterilized, disposable nurser kit

- [ ] Special nursing needs—Pads, etc.

- [ ] Pacifier—Silicone types store much longer than the latex type.

- [ ] Pediatric oral/rectal thermometer

- [ ] Cotton balls, Q-tip applicators

- [ ] Extra crib bedsheets

- [ ] Extra baby blankets and comforters. Consider one or two wool blankets also.

- [ ] Small rubberized bedsheet

- [ ] Bath towels, washcloths

- [ ] Baby socks, booties, shoes

- [ ] Baby cap, mittens

- [ ] Baby coat, sweaters, shirts, undershirts, and sleepers

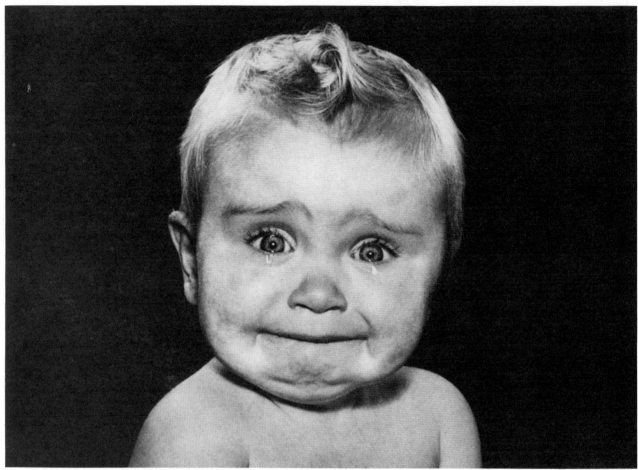

"*Let every head of every household see to it that he has on hand enough food and clothing, and, where possible, fuel also, for at least a year ahead.*

"*. . . We urge you to do this prayerfully and DO IT NOW. I speak with a feeling of great urgency. I have seen what the days of tribulation can do to people. I have seen hunger stalk the streets of Europe. I have witnessed the appalling, emaciated shadows of human figures. I have seen women and children scavage army dumps for scraps of food. Those scenes and nameless faces cannot be erased from my memory.*

"*I shall never forget the Saints of Hamburg who appeared on the verge of collapse from starvation, or their small children whom I invited to the stand as we emptied our pockets of edibles. Most had never seen these items before because of the wartime conditions. Nor can I forget the expectant and nursing mothers whose eyes watered with tears when we gave them each an orange.*

"*We saw the terrible physical and social side effects of hunger and malnutrition. One sister walked over a thousand miles with four small children, leaving her home in Poland. She lost all four to starvation and the freezing conditions. Yet she stood before us in her emaciated condition, her clothing shredded, and her feet wrapped in burlap, and bore testimony of how blessed she was.*" (Ezra Taft Benson, October Conference 1980.)

FUEL HEAT AND LIGHT

- **Materials for alternate heating, lighting, and cooking should be stored to last at least one year. Choose heating, lighting, and cooking equipment that will operate on the same fuel if you prefer convenience in storing and using.**

- Consider investing in a good wood or coal burning stove that serves for heating, cooking, and lighting. Wood stoves are far more efficient heaters than fireplaces.

- Be sure your stove or fireplace and chimney systems are safe and functioning properly.

- A fireplace burning uses about 300 cubic feet of fresh air per minute. Therefore, open a window slightly to allow for adequate ventilation.

- On a wood stove (or regular stove), put on a teapot of water on low heat to produce steam to humidify your home. You will feel much more comfortable (especially with the drying effect of an indoor fire) and will require less actual heat to feel warm and cozy.

- Toss dried orange and lemon rinds into your fireplace for a spicy aroma.

- ☐ **If you have a fireplace, a wood/coal stove, you will want to store several cords of firewood.** Firewood is usually sold by the cord which is a neat pile that totals 128 cubic feet. This pile is four feet wide, four feet high, and eight feet long. Some dealers sell wood by the ton. As a general rule of thumb, a standard cord of air dry dense hardwood weighs about two tons and provides as much heat as one ton of coal. Be suspicious of any alleged cord delivered in a ½ or ¾ ton pick-up truck.

- For best results, wood should be seasoned (dried) properly, usually at least for a year. A plastic tarp, wood planks, or other plastic or metal sheeting over the woodpile is useful in keeping the wood dry.

- Firewood may be obtained inexpensively from orchards being torn down, old buildings being torn down, scrap wood from furniture mills, and even the town dump is a good source of wood.

- **Firewoods rated good to excellent include:** red and white oak; yellow, black and white (paper) birch; sugar maple; red gum; ash; basswood; tulip poplar; cherry; walnut; pinyons; mahogany; eucalyptus; dogwood; hickory; black locust; apple; blue beech; and pine. Check with your local forest service for the best firewoods in your area.

- According to an anonymous English poet:
  Beechwood fires are bright and clear
  If the logs are kept a year.
  Chestnut only good, they say,
  If for long 'tis laid away.
  But ash new or ash old
  Is fit for queen with crown of gold.

  Birch and fir logs burn too fast,
  Blaze up bright and do not last.
  It is by the Irish said
  Hawthorn bakes the sweestest bread.
  Elm wood burns like churchyard mold,
  E'en the very flames are cold.
  But ash green or ash brown
  Is fit for queen with golden crown.

  Poplar gives a bitter smoke,
  Fills your eyes and makes you choke.
  Apple wood will scent your room
  With an incense like perfume.
  Oaken logs, if dry and old,
  Keep away the winter's cold.
  But ash wet or ash dry,
  A king shall warm his slippers by.

- Presto logs are useful for storage. They are comprised of compressed sawdust.

- Newspaper logs can be made by rolling a section of newspaper up to a width of about six inches, soaking it in detergent water, and then standing on end, letting them dry. Pound for pound, newspaper logs are as efficient as wood.

- **Necessary tools for firewood may include:**

☐ Swedish bowsaw

☐ Chainsaws, extra fuel

☐ A couple of wedges

☐ A good splitting hammer (six to twelve pound head)

☐ Axes can be used for splitting, but skill is required

☐ Fireplace tools

☐ **A year's supply of coal should be stored if your stove uses it.**

- Two kinds of coal are used for heating homes—anthracitic is the best type (hard) and more is available in the Eastern U.S., and bituminous (soft).

- Coal may be stored in a plastic-lined pit or in sheds, bags, boxes, or barrels and should be kept away from circulating air, light, and moisture.

☐ **365 candles** of all sizes. The larger the better. 50-hour candles are available in solid and liquid form.

☐ Candle lanterns or broad-based candle holders

- White or light colored candles burn brighter than dark candles.

- Tallow candles burn brighter, longer, and are fairly smoke free when compared to wax candles.

- Candles burn more slowly and evenly and with minimum wax drippings if you place them in the freezer for several hours before using them.

- Aluminum foil placed around a candle in a fan shape will reflect additional light.

- Do not let children carry fuel, lanterns, or lighted candles.

☐ **Several flashlights** — One for each area of the home.

☐ Extra flashlight bulbs. The brightest bulbs are the krypton and halogen type.

☐ Extra alkaline batteries, not only for your flashlight and transistor radio, but for other items in your home which are or can be battery operated. They have a three to five-year shelf-life if stored in cool location and in an airtight container.

☐ Lithium batteries — These store twice as long as alkaline batteries (about ten years).

☐ Rechargable batteries

☐ Charcoal briquettes — The best time to buy briquettes inexpensively is at the end of the summer. Broken or torn bags of briquettes are usually sold at a big discount. Store these outside or inside in metal, airtight containers such as metal trash cans.

☐ Charcoal lighter fluid

☐ Hibachi grill — Use only outside

☐ Charcoal grill

- A charcoal grill gives off more carbon monoxide than a car's engine; therefore, do not use one indoors.

- Charcoal briquettes can also be used in a homemade reflector-type oven made of aluminum foil wrapper inside a cardboard box. Each briquette generates about 40°F. of heat.

☐ **Kerosene lanterns** — 45 hours burning time per quart

☐ White gas lanterns — Outside use only

☐ Propane lantern

☐ Floating wick lanterns made with cooking oil — These can be easily constructed if other type lanterns are unavailable

- A double mantle lantern gives off as much light as two 100-watt light bulbs.

☐ Aladdin lamp — Burns very bright and very hot

- Fashion a tomato cage over an Aladdin lamp to help prevent toppling over and breaking and to help keep children away from the 750°F. heat produced.

☐ Extra wicks, chimneys and mantles for lamps

☐ Kerosene stove and/or heater

- Some kerosene stoves can be used for heating, lighting and cooking.

☐ **Storage kerosene fuel** — Buy only K-1 rating

- Kerosene fuel should be stored according to local laws and regulations. Strict precautions should be observed for safe storage and use.

☐ Propane fueled stove and heater

☐ Storage propane fuel

☐ Catalytic heaters — Light these outside as they flame up several feet when lit. Use them only in well ventilated rooms.

☐ Small camping stoves

☐ Homemade tin can stoves (made from #10 tin can)

☐ Canned heat (Ethanol fuel)

☐ Home power generator (expensive but useful)

☐ Cyalume chemical light sticks — Up to 12 hours of lighting.

☐ Firestarters of various kinds

☐ **Plenty of stick matches** (waterproofed)

☐ Cigarette butane lighters to light candles, lanterns and fireplace.

☐ Extra fuses (if your home has a fusebox)

☐ Extra light bulbs

☐ Hot water bottle (rubber)

- A hot water bottle can also be made by filling a quart size canning jar or plastic container up with hot water and wrapping in a towel. It helps keep the feet toasty warm in the cold.

☐ Heavy plastic sheeting to cover windows in winter

☐ Weatherstripping materials

- Save old phone books, magazines, newspapers and grocery sacks for emergency fuels

☐ **At least two battery-operated smoke detectors should be in your home. Suggested is one each of the ionization type and the photoelectric type on each separate level of your home. Store extra batteries for them.**

☐ **One or two ABC-type fire extinguishers** are also essential, especially when the fireplace and lanterns and various type heaters are used often.

☐ **Fire escape ladder for second story of home**

☐ Several lengths of garden hose should be hooked up and ready to use for fighting fires. It should be long enough to reach anywhere in your home.

☐ A waterbucket (by the fireplace)

• **Light all cooking, heating and lighting equipment outdoors or by a window that is open several inches.**

• **Carbon monoxide kills quietly. Ventilate closed quarters heated by any open flame heater, even a candle or lantern. Vent near the roof and the floor.**

The powerful Mexico City earthquake registered 7.8 on the Richter Scale and last four nightmarish minutes. Skyscrapers swayed as far north as Houston, Texas, 1,100 miles from the epicenter.

The disaster left over 80,000 people homeless in the capital alone. Pictured are several young homeless children near a pile of rubble in what used to be their home.

Mexico City earthquake, September 1985, Cuidad Guzman, Mexico. American Red Cross photo.

EMERGENCY FUELS, SAFETY CONSIDERATIONS

by Tom Wroe, Fire Marshal,
Utah County Sheriff's Office, Provo, Utah
December 1987
(Reprinted by permission)

An emergency situation will cause a myriad of problems in individual homes. The most primitive concerns become the most important for survival—shelter (warmth), clothing, and food (cooking). We take these things for granted for the most part, but should the situation arise, these items will rise to the top of our hierarchy of needs.

In our preparation for disasters and local emergencies, we consider the amount of food, clothing and, where possible, fuel to sustain us for one year. It is suggested to counsel with your family to determine your needs for survival. It may not be possible to maintain the same level of comfort you now enjoy. However, there are several things that should be done to reduce the danger sure to arise if we start using unusual methods for survival.

We are governed by laws established to protect us from hazards. In storing fuels for heat, cooking and light, the most important recommendation is to check with local authorities regarding the requirements of storing flammable and combustible materials. "Illegal" storage can possibly result in voiding insurance contracts.

The definition of a **flammable** liquid is basically a liquid that has a flash point less than 100 degrees Fahrenheit. Liquids with a flash point greater than 100 degrees Fahrenheit are considered **combustible** liquids. This is an over simplification but satisfactory for this discussion.

Storing flammable and combustible liquids is very hazardous and can be deadly. During the late 1970s, when gasoline was thought to be in short supply, a family was storing gas in a 40 gallon plastic trash can in their closet near the front door. A fire occurred when attempting to transfer gas using a canister vacuum cleaner. The results were devastating!

The first rule of thumb is **DO NOT** store flammable or combustible liquids in **ANY** living space. This includes any storage room. These materials increase the intensity of fire. Vapors given off can be ignited by open flames in water heaters, furnaces, and also from electric sources.

Burning inside today's modern homes can be more hazardous than older homes. This is due to:

1. Construction techniques that more effectively "seal" a building for insulation purposes.

2. Lowering of building standards allowing 2"x4" trusses rather than 2"x6" construction which presents an additional hazard to firefighters.

3. The increased use of plastics.

The result is a greater build up of heat, potential structural failure, and the retention of toxic gases. The products of combustion of any heat source is of greatest concern in a home. Your gas fired furnace, water heater, and stove are provided with a vent to the outside of the building. Additionally, your fireplace and wood burning stove have a chimney. The reason is simply to prevent the accumulation of toxic gases inside the building.

The products of combustion are **ALWAYS** going to include: Carbon Dioxide, Carbon Monoxide, Sulfur Dioxide, Nitrogen Dioxide, Hydrogen, and water. Other building contents (plastics) will emit Hydrogen Chloride or Hydrogen Cyanide. (Hydrogen Cyanide is used in gas chambers for executions.)

The amounts of toxic gases produced will vary greatly depending on the type of fuel, the burning rate, and BTU capacity. The exact amount of toxic gases cannot be precisely calculated without considering the exact room size, construction, fuel, and appliance. **EXTREME CARE SHOULD BE GIVEN WHEN CONSIDERING ANY FIRE INSIDE A BUILDING.** It is very possible that lives will be lost!

According to the 1985 Uniform Mechanical Code:

> Unvented fuel-burning room heaters **shall not** be installed, used, maintained or permitted to exist in any Group "I" (Institutional) or "R" (Residential) Occupancy nor shall any such heater be installed in any building, whether as a new or as a replacement installation. . . . (Sec. 807C)

The Uniform Fire Code requires a formal **permit** from the local Fire Prevention Bureau to store the following:

Cryogen is defined as a substance having a low temperature. (An example is LPG or Propane stored under pressure as a liquid and "boils" at -44°F.) Any amount over 1 gallon stored inside a building or 60 gallons stored outside.

Flammable or Combustible Liquids

a. To store, handle or use Class I Flammable liquids (such as gasoline) in excess of 5 gallons in a building or in excess of 10 gallons outside.

b. To store, handle or use Class II (such as Kerosene) or Class III Combustible liquids (such as Lubricating Oil for your car) in excess of 25 gallons in a building or 60 gallons outside. The exception is fuel used in connection with oil-burning equipment.

SOLID FUELS

Other considerations are wood, coal and charcoal. Wood piles should be located a safe distance away from the house. Try to keep no more than two or three day's supply in the house located a safe distance from the fireplace or stove.

Coal should only be burned in a stove/furnace designed for high temperatures. Coal is susceptible to rapid deterioration when exposed to light and moisture. Often, coal is kept in a covered container or in a covered pit. Low sulfur coal is preferable and reduces the amount of sulfur dioxide. It should be noted that sulfur dioxide chemically combines with water vapors to form sulfuric acid. This same phenomenon occurs on your car exhaust system causing it to decay.

Charcoal should **NEVER** be burned inside a building due to high levels of Carbon Monoxide gas produced. Indoor storage of charcoal should be in metal cans with a tight fitting lid. Charcoal will spontaneously ignite by absorbing sufficient moisture that will initiate a chemical (endothermic) reaction, and this type of container will help prevent this occurrence.

LIQUID AND GAS FUELS

Gasoline is typically used for use in vehicles, lawn equipment, and in electric generators. This is a very volatile fuel that should **never** be stored in a living space or in basements. There are very strict regulations in storing flammable liquids, and advice from your local authorities is recommended.

Kerosene is common as a heating and light fuel throughout the world. The dangers of portable kerosene heaters have been well documented and known for years. The major concerns are spills due to the heater being tipped over or being placed too close to other combustible materials. Not all of these devices comply with even minimum standards nor are they properly UL listed. However, are UL listed heaters really safe? UL Standard 647, first formulated in 1924, is frequently used and allows 30 seconds for flame extinction upon tip-over and also permits some fuel leakage.

The newer models are less likely to tip over and typically have an automatic shut-off in the event it does tip. However, this is a mechanical action and several heaters have failed due to improper replacement parts or carbon built up due to improper fuel.

Kerosene (also known as Range Oil No. 1) is a combustible liquid and has a flash point between 101 °F. and 130 °F. This is due to the varying hydrocarbon composition. **Caution** should be given to buying only low sulfur fuel (designated "1K").

The result is a lower emission of Sulfur Dioxide and less damage to the heater and wick. Remember, parts of the heater reach temperatures well above the ignition temperature of the fuel and spills will self-ignite.

Underwriters Laboratories (UL), when approving a Kerosene heater, limits the production of Carbon Monoxide to 40 parts per million (ppm). EPA has set a standard of 9 ppm as the maximum safe exposure when exceeding an 8 hour period. The UL limits for Carbon Dioxide is 80 ppm. Much higher levels can be reached. Nitrogen Dioxide up to 2 ppm (EPA **annual** pollution average in air allowable is 0.5 ppm.), and Sulfur Dioxide up to 10 ppm were recorded. (EPA has established a safe level of 0.14 ppm during a 24 hour period.) These products of combustion are highly toxic and will cause unconsciousness and death when accumulations exceed allowable levels.

The question of how much air or how far to open a window or door to make up for the lack of oxygen in the room is not easily answered. When dealing with poisonous gases such as Carbon Monoxide, Sulfur Dioxide, or Nitrogen Dioxide, an incorrect calculation could be fatal.

Propane is a highly flammable cryogen used generally for heating and cooking purposes. It also can be used for light. The greatest concern with this gas, being heavier than air, is "pooling" which can create an explosive atmosphere.

Advertisers claim the products of combustion of Propane are Carbon Dioxide and water. They fail to recognize the presence of the other gases formed which are dependent upon the proper working condition of the devices. When Oxygen in a room is depleted during combustion, the efficiency of any device diminishes and even more Carbon Monoxide is formed. Additionally, for each gallon of propane burned, approximately 0.8 gallons of water vapor is formed that can be very damaging to walls, wood, and can be corrosive to metal.

Some heating units are equipped with an ODS (Oxygen Depletion Sensor) that shuts off the fuel supply when the Oxygen to the pilot drops to 18%. This mechanical device is highly susceptible to malfunction, and you might be betting your life on it.

Storage of propane greater than one gallon must be outside, a sufficient distance from buildings and property lines. **Consult** your local authorities for these details. A permit is also required for the installation and storage of bulk amounts of Propane and is not permitted in below grade rooms.

Basement natural gas heating units **CANNOT** be legally converted for Propane use. Again, the vapors are heavier than air and form "pockets." Ignition sources such as water heaters and electrical sources can cause an explosion.

Kerosene lanterns are another consideration. Without electricity, another source of light will be necessary. Besides flashlights, there are some good and efficient lanterns available and all have one thing in common. They produce products of combustion including heat. The amount of toxic vapors are much less than heaters.

Due to a slower burning rate, they may still need to be ventilated. **Never** leave a lantern burning unattended or while you are sleeping.

With temperatures up to 500°F. produced, these devices can quickly and easily start a fire. Manufactures recommend at least 36" clearance above and around most lanterns and heaters. There is a possibility of pyrophoric action to wood cabinets. This is the charring of wood without combustion and essentially is how charcoal is made.

White gas should **NEVER** be used inside your home. It is very unsafe and explosive. Treat it the same as you would gasoline. Toxic vapors, including high levels of Carbon Monoxide, can be experienced.

Candles are available for up to 50 hours of use. Any open flame can be hazardous and should be considered carefully. A substantial base for the candle should be provided so that if the candle does fall over, the container will contain the entire candle. Locate it where children can't get to it or it to them and **never** leave children unattended with a burning device.

As a summary, **remember:**

. . . **any** burning device inside your home must be properly vented and located a safe distance from combustible materials for the safety of you and your family.

. . . A properly serviced "ABC" fire extinguisher should be provided as part of your preparation for emergencies. This class extinguisher can be used on **any** fire in the home. Additionally, products of combustion smoke detectors should be installed to provide an early warning should a fire occur.

. . . Your home must be protected from the ravages of fire by your actions. Study the instructions for your appliances and understand their features as well as their limitations.

. . . Don't go to sleep with any unvented burning device in your home. Your family might not wake up.

. . . Whatever you store, store it **safely** and **legally**.

. . . In an emergency, survival may cause you to make decisions that are questionable with regard to safety. Become educated to the inherent hazards of your choices and make a decision based on as much verifiable information as possible. You and your family's lives will depend on it.

For additional specific information, contact your local authorities.

During an earthquake try to stay calm. The roaring and rolling can be very terrifying, but unless something falls on you, the earthquake probably won't hurt you. If you're indoors, stay there. Get under a heavy table or desk to protect yourself from falling debris or move into a doorway or against inside walls. A door frame or the structural frame of the building are its strongest points and are least likely to collapse. Always stay away from windows; the rocking motion of an earthquake may shatter them.

Streets that collapsed in downtown Anchorage during the 1964 Alaskan earthquake (magnitude 8.5). Photo courtesy of U.S. Geological Survey.

Following a major disaster, your local fire department may be overwhelmed with calls for assistance. They may be unable to respond to small residential fires (frequently caused by arcing wires, downed electrical lines, or damaged wiring in appliances). Having multi-purpose dry chemical A-B-C fire extinguishers and knowing how to use them is a must for every family.

In addition to fire extinguishers, properly installed smoke detectors save lives. Since most fire deaths are caused by asphyxiation, early warning of a fire could prevent these deaths from occurring. A smoke detector could also warn you if a fire breaks out when you are sleeping.

Since fire is the most likely disaster family members are likely to experience, a well-rehearsed family fire escape plan is absolutely necessary. (Photo courtesy of the Los Angeles City Fire Department.)

SUGGESTED BOOKS AND PUBLICATIONS

- *An Enemy Hath Done This*
  by Ezra Taft Benson

- *On Wings of Faith*
  by Fred Babbel

- *Outdoor Survival Skills*
  by Larry Dean Olson

- *Nuclear War Survival Skills*
  by Cresson H. Kearny

- *Fieldbook*
  Boy Scouts of America

  Following are Boy Scout Merit Badge pamphlets:
  Emergency Preparedness
  Wilderness Survival
  Firemanship
  Gardening
  Camping
  Cooking
  First Aid
  Home Repairs
  Fruit and Nut Growing

- *Advanced First Aid*
  American Red Cross

- *In Time of Emergency . . . A Citizen's Handbook*
  38 pages
  Available free from
  Federal Emergency Management Agency
  Washington, D.C. 20472

- "Essentials of Home Production and Storage"
  Available for 50 cents at the
  LDS Distribution Center
  Salt Lake City, Utah

- "Preparing for and Responding To Emergencies:
  Guidelines for Church Leaders"
  Available for no charge at the
  LDS Distribution Center
  Salt Lake City, Utah

- The following publications are available from the Ezra Taft Benson Agriculture and Food Institute, Brigham Young University, Provo, Utah 84602:

  1. *Having Your Food Storage and Eating It, Too*
     Nominal fee

  2. *Eating Right and Enjoying Life More*
     Nominal fee

  3. *Getting Along with Your Garden*
     Nominal fee

- *72-Hour Family Emergency Preparedness Checklist*
  by Barry and Lynette Crockett
  $8.95, plus $2.00 postage
  Box 1601
  Orem, Utah 84059

- The following U.S. Government Publications are available by writing:
  Government Printing Office
  710 North Capitol Street, NW
  Washington, DC 20401
  Phone: (202) 275-2091

HOME AND GARDEN BULLETINS

(G-8) *Home Canning of Fruits and Vegetables* ($1.50)

(G-10) *Home Freezing of Fruits and Vegetables* ($2.00)

(G-56) *How to Make Jellies, Jams, and Preserves at Home* ($2.50)

(G-92) *Making Pickles and Relishes at Home* ($2.00)

(G-106) *Home Canning of Meat and Poultry* ($2.25)

(G-119) *Storing Vegetables and Fruits in Basements, Cellars, Outbuildings, and Pits* ($2.25)

(G-162) *Keeping Food Safe to Eat: A Guide for Homemakers* ($1.00)

(G-163) *Minigardens for Vegetables* ($2.25)

(G-185) *Mulches for Your Garden* ($1.00)

(G-202) *Growing Vegetables in the Home Garden* ($3.25)

(G-208) *Soybeans in Family Meals: A Guide for Consumers* ($3.50)

(G-211) *Control of Insects on Deciduous Fruits and Tree Nuts in the Home Orchard* ($2.00)

(AB-380) *Insects and Diseases of Vegetables in the Home Garden* ($4.25)

(HERR-46) *Meat, Poultry, Fish and Eggs: Selection, Storage, and Preparation* ($1.50)

(L-407) *Dwarf Fruit Trees — Selection and Care* ($2.00)

(L-559) *Firewood for Your Fireplace: Selection, Purchase, Use* ($1.00)

(PA-1034) *Simple Home Repairs — Inside* ($1.75)

(PA-1193) *Simple Home Repairs — Outside* ($2.00)

- The following booklet is available for free by writing to:

  S. James
  Consumer Information Center-F
  P.O. Box 100
  Pueblo, Colorado 81002

  Consumer's Guide To Food Labels
  Explains dating, symbols, grades, and nutrition information on food labels.

After a hurricane warning has been issued, precautionary actions should be taken immediately:

1. *Moor boats securely or evacuate them to a safer area. When the boat is moored, leave it and don't return while the wind and waves are up.*
2. *Board over windows or protect them with storm shutters or tape. For small windows, the main danger comes from wind-driven debris, but larger windows may be broken by the pressure of the intense winds.*
3. *Secure any outdoor objects that might be blown away or uprooted. This includes garbage cans, garden tools, toys, porch furniture, and signs. In addition, there are many objects that seem completely harmless until a hurricane-force wind strikes them, and they become as deadly as a wartime missile.*
4. *Move valuables, including food storage, to upper floors.*

In this photo, a rather large fishing boat was blown into a home from the intense winds of Hurricane Camille in Biloxi, Mississippi (August 1969). For scale, note the two individuals sitting on the back of the boat. (Photo courtesy of the National Oceanic and Atmospheric Administration.)

STATEMENTS BY THE BRETHREN

The following sampling of quotes from Church leaders over the years are intended to be used for reference on the subject of preparedness, a year's supply, and self-reliance. It is hoped that addresses will be looked up and studied in their entirety to ensure proper contextual meaning of passages and to derive a fuller understanding of the principle of self-reliance.

Ezra Taft Benson
October Conference, 1952

I thought, too, of our visits to other cities—to Frankfurt, Frieburg, Hamburg, Hanover, and our first visit to Berlin. The three and one-half hour meeting with the Saints in Berlin will never be forgotten, nor shall I forget my feelings as we looked into the faces of refugees who had come across country on foot from Poland—people half-starved, with all their earthly belongings on their backs, and yet with the light of truth and faith in God shining in their eyes.

. . . I remember, too, my brethren and sisters, when the first Church welfare supplies arrived in Berlin. I presume you have never had the great and trying experience of looking into the faces of people who are starving when you are unable to give them even a crust of bread. We faced that as we first met with the Saints in parts of Europe.

But when the welfare supplies came, it was a time never to be forgotten by these faithful Saints. I can see them now in tears, weeping like children, as they looked upon those first boxes of welfare supplies when they reached occupied Germany.

. . . I remember our meeting with the Saints way up in East Prussia, near the Russian border, Saints who had known slave labor, who had suffered indescribable privation and hardship, worse than death, and yet whose faith and whose testimonies were still burning brightly.

. . . I remember, my brethren and sisters, great tracts of once fertile and productive land lying idle. The anomaly of land idle, and people starving because there was no seed to plant, no machinery with which to plant, cultivate, and harvest, and no power because power machines had been destroyed and horses had been killed during the bombing and many others killed and eaten for human's food! All these and many other things have passed through my mind the last few days as we have been assembled here in conference.

The aftermath of the war is usually worse than the actual physical combat. Everywhere there is the suffering of old people, innocent women and children. Economies are broken down, the spirits of people crushed, men and women bewildered and a spirit of frustration prevails. It is a saddening thing to see people who have lost their freedom—the right to choose—who have lost their right to move about freely, to assemble together as we meet here today. I recalled, too, the sin and corruption, the immorality and the starvation that always follow war.

. . . I came to know, my brethren and sisters, through the lives of our Saints abroad, that men and women who have a testimony of this work can endure anything which they may be called upon to endure and still keep sweet in spirit.

The Saints in Europe taught me a new appreciation for the priesthood of God. I heard them bear testimony of their gratitude for the priesthood in their homes. Many families who had been isolated from other representatives of the priesthood during the bombing and during sickness told of their gratitude that they had in their homes the authority and the power to lay their hands upon members of their families, and under the inspiration of heaven invoke God's healing power upon them.

* * * * * *

Ezra Taft Benson
April Conference, 1965

For years we have been counseled to have on hand a year's supply of food. Yet there are some today who would not start storing until the Church comes out with a detailed monthly home storage program. Now suppose that never happens? We still cannot say we have not been told.

Should the Lord decide at this time to cleanse the Church . . . a famine in this land of one year's duration could wipe out a large percentage of slothful members, including some ward and stake officers. Yet we cannot say we have not been warned.

* * * * * *

Ezra Taft Benson
October Conference, 1973

What are some of the calamities for which we are to prepare? In section 29 the Lord warns us of "a great hailstorm sent forth to destroy the crops of the earth." (D&C 29:16.) In section 45 we read of "an overflowing scourge; for a desolating sickness shall cover the land." (D&C 45:31.) In section 63 the Lord declares he has "decreed wars upon the face of the earth. . . ." (D&C 63:33.)

In Matthew, chapter 24, we learn of "famines, and pestilences, and earthquakes. . . ." (Matt. 24:7.) The Lord declared that these and other calamities shall occur. These particular prophecies seem not to be conditional. The Lord, with his foreknowledge, knows that they will happen. Some will come about through man's manipulations; others through the forces of nature and nature's God, but that they will come seems certain. Prophecy is but history in reverse—a divine disclosure of future events.

Yet, through all of this, the Lord Jesus Christ has said: ". . . if ye are prepared ye shall not fear." (D&C 38:30.)

. . . Here then is the key—look to the prophets for the words of God, that will show us how to prepare for the calamities which are to come.

. . . For the righteous the gospel provides a warning before a calamity, a program for the crises, a refuge for each disaster.

. . . The Lord has warned us of famines, but the righteous will have listened to prophets and stored at least a year's supply of survival food.

. . . The Lord desires his Saints to be free and independent in the critical days ahead. But no man is truly free who is in financial bondage. "Think what you do when you run in debt," said Benjamin Franklin, "you give to another power over your liberty. ". . . pay thy debt and live . . ." said Elisha. (2 Kings 4:7.) And in the Doctrine and Covenants the Lord says, ". . . it is my will that you shall pay all your debts." (D&C 104:78.)

For over 100 years we have been admonished to store up grain. "Remember the counsel that is given," said Elder Orson Hyde, "'. . . *Store up all your grain*,' and take care of it! . . . And I tell you it is almost as necessary to have bread to sustain the body as it is to have food for the spirit; for the one is as necessary as the other to enable us to carry on the work of God upon the earth." (*Journal of Discourses*, vol. 5, p. 17.) And he also said: "There is more salvation and security in wheat, than in all the political schemes of the world . . . ." (*JD*, vol. 2, p. 207.)

. . . As to the foodstuffs which should be stored, the Church has left that decision primarily to the individual members. Some excellent suggestions are available from the Church Welfare Committee. "All grain is good for the food of man. . ." (D&C 89:16) the Lord states, but he particularly singles out wheat. Dry, whole, hard grains, when stored properly, can last indefinitely, and their nutritional value can be enhanced through sprouting, if desired.

It would be well if every family have on hand grain for at least a year.

From the standpoint of food production, storage, handling, and the Lord's counsel, wheat should have high priority. Water, of course, is essential. Other basics could include honey or sugar, legumes, milk products or substitutes, and salt or its equivalent. The revelation to store food may be as essential to our temporal salvation today as boarding the ark was to the people in the days of Noah.

President Harold B. Lee has wisely counseled that "perhaps if we think not in terms of a year's supply of what we ordinarily would use, and think more in terms of what it would take to keep us alive in case we didn't have anything else to eat, that last would be very easy to put in storage for a year . . . just enough to keep us alive if we didn't have anything else to eat. We wouldn't get fat on it, but we would live; and if you think in terms of that kind of annual storage rather than a whole year's supply of everything that you are accustomed to eat which, in most cases, is utterly impossible for the average family, I think we will come nearer to what President Clark advised us way back in 1937." (Welfare conference address, October 1, 1966.)

. . . There are blessings in being close to the soil, in raising your own food, even if it is only a garden in your yard and/or a fruit tree or two.

. . . Those families will be fortunate who, in the last days, have an adequate supply of each of these particulars.

. . . Concerning clothing, we should anticipate future needs, such as extra work clothes and clothes that would supply warmth during winter months when there may be shortages or lack of heating fuel. Leather and bolts of cloth could be stored, particularly for families with younger children who will outgrow and perhaps outwear their present clothes.

"The day will come," said President Wilford Woodruff, "when, as we have been told, we shall all see the necessity of making our own shoes and clothing and raising our own food. . . ." (*Discourses of Wilford Woodruff*, p. 166.)

. . . In a message to the Saints in July of 1970, President Joseph Fielding Smith stated that the pioneers "were taught by their leaders to produce, as far as possible, all that they consumed. . . This is still excellent counsel." (*Improvement Era*, vol. 73 [1970], p. 3.)

Wood, coal, gas, oil, kerosene, and even candles are among those items which could be reserved as fuel for warmth, cooking, and light or power. Some may be used for all of these purposes and certain ones would have to be stored and handled cautiously. It would also be well to have on hand some basic medical supplies to last for at least a year.

. . . The Saints have been advised to pay their own way and maintain a cash reserve. Recent history has demonstrated that in difficult days it is reserves with intrinsic value that are of most worth, rather than reserves, the value of which may be destroyed through inflation. It is well to remember that continued government deficits cause inflation; inflation is used as an excuse for ineffective price controls; price controls lead to shortages; artificial shortages inevitably are used as an excuse to implement rationing.

When will we learn these basic economic principles? However, ". . . when we really get into hard times," said President Clark, "where food is scarce or there is none at all, and so with clothing and shelter, money may be no good for there may be nothing to buy, and you cannot eat money, you cannot get enough of it together to burn to keep warm, and you cannot wear it." (*Church News,* November 21, 1953, p. 4.)

. . . "How on the face of the earth could a man enjoy his religion," said Elder George A. Smith many years ago, "when he had been told by the Lord how to prepare for a day of famine, when, instead of doing so, he had fooled away that which would have sustained him and his family." (*JD*, vol. 12, p. 142.)

And President Brigham Young said, "If you are without bread, how much wisdom can you boast, and of what real utility are your talents, if you cannot procure for yourselves and save against a day of scarcity those substances designed to sustain your natural lives? . . . If you cannot provide for your natural lives, how can you expect to have wisdom to obtain eternal lives?" (*JD*, vol. 8, p. 68.)

. . . When will all these calamities strike? We do not know the exact time, but it appears it may be in the not-too-distant future. Those who are prepared now have the continuing blessings of early obedience, and they are ready. Noah built his ark before the flood came, and he and his family survived. Those who waited to act until after the flood began were too late.

Let us not be dissuaded from preparing because of a seeming prosperity today, or a so-called peace.

I have seen the ravages of inflation. I shall never forget Germany in the early 1920s. In December 1923 in Cologne, Germany, I paid six billion marks for breakfast. That was just 15 cents in American money. Today, the real inflation concern is in America and several other nations.

. . . I have witnessed with my own eyes the ravages of hunger and destitution as, under the direction of the president of the Church, I spent a year in war-torn Europe at the close of World War II, without my family, distributing food, clothing, and bedding to our needy members. I have looked into the sunken eyes of Saints, in almost the last stages of starvation. I have seen faithful mothers carrying their children, three and four years of age, who were unable to walk because of malnutrition. I have seen a hungry woman turn down food for a spool of thread. I have seen grown men weep as they ran their hands through the wheat and beans sent to them from Zion—America.

Thanks be to God for a prophet, for this inspired program, and for Saints who so managed their stewardship that they could provide for their own and still share with others. What a marvelous way to become a savior on Mount Zion!

. . . May we ever remember the Lord's promise: ". . . if ye are prepared ye shall not fear." (D&C 38:30.)

. . . The days ahead are sobering and challenging. Oh, may we be prepared spiritually and temporally. . . .

*　*　*　*　*　*

Ezra Taft Benson
April Conference, 1977

Economic and social conditions appear most ominous worldwide today. With revelation and prophecy as our guide, I think it is not extreme for me to say that when all is written about our present generation, it may truly be said that we had hardly enough time to prepare. To meet the impending crisis, I venture to say that all our spiritual and temporal resources will be taxed to the very limit. The Lord has declared: "If ye are prepared ye shall not fear." (D&C 38:30.)

. . . Great blessings come to us as individuals and to His Church as we support the Lord's program for the care of the poor and needy. I have experienced these blessings firsthand in distributing food, clothing, and bedding to the suffering members of the Church in Europe following World War II. I witnessed the starving, the emaciated, and the barefoot. It was a piteous sight. My heart went out in compassion to all our Heavenly Father's suffering children.

I remember so well the arrival of our first Church welfare supplies in Berlin. I took with me the acting president of the mission, President Richard Ranglack. We walked to the old battered warehouse which, under armed guard, housed the precious welfare goods. At the far end of the warehouse we saw the boxes piled almost to the ceiling.

"Are those boxes of food?" Richard said. "Do you mean to tell me those are boxes full of food?"

"Yes, my brother," I replied, "food and clothing and bedding—and, I hope, a few medical supplies."

Richard and I took down one of the boxes. We opened it. It was filled with the commonest of common foods—dried beans. As that good man saw it, he put his hands into it and ran it through his fingers, than broke down and cried like a child with gratitude.

We opened another box, filled with cracked wheat, nothing added or taken away, just as the Lord made it and intended it to be. He touched a pinch of it to his mouth. After a moment he looked at me through his tearful eyes—and mine were wet, too—and he said, while slowly shaking his head, "Brother Benson, it is hard to believe that people who have never seen us could do so much for us."

*　*　*　*　*　*

Ezra Taft Benson
October Conference, 1979

The truth is, we have to a great extent accommodated ourselves to Communism—and we have permitted ourselves to become encircled by its tentacles. Though we give lip service to the Monroe Doctrine, this has not prevented Cuba from becoming a Soviet military base, ninety miles off our coastline, nor has it prevented the takeover of Nicaragua in Central America, the surrender of the Panama Canal, or the infiltration by enemy agents within our American borders.

Never before has the land of Zion appeared so vulnerable to so powerful an enemy as the Americas do at present. And our vulnerability is directly attributable to our loss of active faith in the God of this land, who has decreed that we must worship Him or be swept off. Too many Americans have lost sight of the truth that God is our source of freedom—the Lawgiver—and that personal righteousness is the most important essential to preserving our freedom. So, I say with all the energy of my soul that unless we as citizens of this nation forsake our sins, political and otherwise, and return to the fundamental principles of Christianity and of constitutional government, we will lose our political liberties, our free institutions, and will stand in jeopardy before God.

No nation which has kept the commandments of God has ever perished, but I say to you that once freedom is lost, only blood—human blood—will win it back.

There are some things we can and must do at once if we are to stave off a holocaust of destruction.

. . . I have seen the Soviet Union, under its godless leaders, spread its ideology throughout the world. Every strategem is used—trade, war, revolution, violence, hate, detente, and immorality—to accomplish its purposes. Many nations are now under its oppressive control. Over one billion people—one-fourth of the population of the world—have now lost their freedom and are under Communist domination. We seem to forget that the great objective of Communism is still world domination and control, which means the surrender of our freedom—your freedom—our sovereignty.

. . . I testify to you that God's hand has been in our destiny. I testify that freedom as we know it today is being threatened as never before in our history.

*   *   *   *   *   *

Ezra Taft Benson
October Conference, 1980

For over forty years, in a spirit of love, members of the Church have been counseled to be thrifty and self-reliant; to avoid debt; pay tithes and a generous fast offering; be industrious; and have sufficient food, clothing, and fuel on hand to last at least one year.

Today there are compelling reasons to reemphasize this counsel.

. . . In saying this, I am aware of and sympathetic to the plight of many young families who are struggling to make ends meet. They are faced with the financial burden of providing for the three great necessities of life: food, clothing, and shelter. I am also sympathetic to the situation of widows and other sisters who rear families alone. By revelation, the Lord made provision for their care and support. (See D&C 83:1-2, 4-6.)

. . . We do know that the Lord has decreed global calamities for the future and has warned and forewarned us to be prepared. For this reason the Brethren have repeatedly stressed a "back to basics" program for temporal and spiritual welfare.

. . . Today, I emphasize a most basic principle: home production and storage. Have you ever paused to realize what would happen to your community or nation if transportation were paralyzed or if we had a war or depression? How would you and your neighbors obtain food? How long would the corner grocery store—or supermarket—sustain the needs of the community?

. . . Shortly after World War II, I was called by the First Presidency to go to Europe to reestablish our missions and set up a program for the distribution of food and clothing to the Saints. Vivid in my memory are the people who got on trains each morning with all kinds of bric-a-brac in their arms to go out to the countryside to trade their possessions for food. At evening time, the train station was filled with people with arms full of vegetables and fruits, and a menagerie of squealing pigs and chickens. You never heard such a commotion. These people were, of course, willing to barter practically anything for the commodity which sustains life—food.

. . . An almost forgotten means of economic self-reliance is the home production of food. We are too accustomed to going to stores and purchasing what we need.

. . . No more timely counsel, I feel, has been given by President Kimball than his repeated emphasis to grow our own gardens. Here is one sample of his emphasis over the past seven years:

"We encourage you to grow all the food that you feasibly can on your own property. Berry bushes, grapevines, fruit trees—plant them if your climate is right for their growth. Grow vegetables and eat them from your own yard." (*Ensign*, May 1976, p. 124.)

Many of you have listened and done as President Kimball counseled, and you have been blessed for it. Others have rationalized that they had no time or space. May I suggest you do what others have done. Get together with others and seek permission to use a vacant lot for a garden, or rent a plot of ground and grow your gardens. Some elders quorums have done this as a quorum, and all who have participated have reaped the benefits of a vegetable and fruit harvest and the blessings of cooperation and family involvement. Many families have dug up lawn space for gardens.

. . . We encourage you to be more self-reliant so that, as the Lord has declared, "notwithstanding the tribulation which shall descend upon you, . . . the church may stand independent above all other creatures beneath the celestial world" (D&C 78:14). The Lord wants us to be independent and self-reliant because these will be days of tribulation. He has warned and forewarned us of the eventuality.

President Brigham Young said, "If you are without bread, how much wisdom can you boast, and of what real utility are your talents, if you cannot procure for yourselves and save against a day of scarcity those substances designed to sustain your natural lives?" (In *Journal of Discourses*, 8:68.)

. . . Food production is just one part of the repeated emphasis that you store a provision of food which will last for at least a year wherever it is legally permissible to do so. The Church has not told you what foods should be stored. This decision is left up to individual members. However, some excellent suggestions are available in the booklet produced by the Church entitled "Essentials of Home Production & Storage" (stock no. PGWE1125; 50 cents each). There are also booklets available on gardening from BYU.

. . . From the standpoint of food production, storage, handling, and the Lord's counsel, wheat should have high priority. "There is more salvation and security in wheat," said Orson Hyde years ago, "than in all the political schemes of the world" (in *Journal of Discourses*, 2:207). Water, of course, is essential. Other basics could include honey or sugar, legumes, milk products or substitutes, and salt or its equivalent.

. . . The revelation to produce and store food may be as essential to our temporal welfare today as boarding the ark was to the people in the days of Noah.

. . . Elder Harold B. Lee counseled, "Perhaps if we think not in terms of a year's supply of what we ordinarily would use, and think more in terms of what it would take to keep us alive in case we didn't have anything else to eat, that last would be very easy to put in storage for a year . . . just enough to keep us alive if we didn't have anything else to eat. We wouldn't get fat on it, but we would live; and if you think in terms of that kind of annual storage rather than a whole year's supply of everything that you are accustomed to eat which, in most cases, is utterly impossible for the average family, I think we will become nearer to what President J. Reuben Clark, Jr., advised us way back in 1937." (In Welfare Conference, 1 October 1966.)

. . . There are blessings in being close to the soil, in raising your own food even if it is only a garden in your yard and a fruit tree or two. Those families will be fortunate who, in the last days, have an adequate supply of food because of their foresight and ability to produce their own.

. . . "Let every head of every household see to it that he has on hand enough food and clothing, and, where possible, fuel also, for at least a year ahead. You of small means put your money in foodstuffs and wearing apparel, not in stocks and bonds; you of large means will think you know how to care for yourselves, but I may venture to suggest that you do not speculate. Let every head of every household aim to own his own home, free from mortgage. Let every man who has a garden spot, garden it; every man who owns a farm, farm it." (President J. Reuben Clark, Jr., in Conference Report, Apr. 1937, p. 26.)

. . . You do not need to go into debt, may I add, to obtain a year's supply. Plan to build up your food supply just as you would a savings account. Save a little for storage each pay-check. Can or bottle fruit and vegetables from your gardens and orchards. Learn how to preserve food through drying and possibly freezing. Make your storage a part of your budget. Store seeds and have sufficient tools on hand to do the job. If you are saving and planning for a second car or a TV set or some item which merely adds to your comfort or pleasure, you may need to change your priorities. We urge you to do this prayerfully and *do it now*.

I speak with a feeling of great urgency. I have seen what the days of tribulation can do to people. I have seen hunger stalk the streets of Europe. I have witnessed the appalling, emaciated shadows of human figures. I have seen women and children scavange army garbage dumps for scraps of food. Those scenes and nameless faces cannot be erased from my memory.

. . . I shall never forget the Saints of Hamburg who appeared on the verge of collapse from starvation, or their small children whom I invited to come to the stand as we emptied our pockets of edibles. Most had never seen these items before because of the wartime conditions. Nor can I forget the expectant and nursing mothers whose eyes watered with tears when we gave them each an orange. We saw the terrible physical and social side effects of hunger and malnutrition. One sister walked over a thousand miles with four small children, leaving her home in Poland. She lost all four to starvation and the freezing conditions. Yet she stood before us in her emaciated condition, her clothing shredded, and her feet wrapped in burlap, and bore testimony of how blessed she was.

. . . Nor will I ever forget the faith of the Dutch Saints who accepted our suggestion to grow potatoes to alleviate their own starving conditions, and then sent a portion of their first harvest to the German people who had been their bitter enemies. The following year they sent them the entire harvest. The annals of Church history have seldom recorded a more Christlike act of love and compassion.

. . . Too often we bask in our comfortable complacency and rationalize that the ravages of war, economic disaster, famine, and earthquake cannot happen here. Those who believe this are either not acquainted with the revelations of the Lord, or they do not believe them. Those who smugly think these calamities will not happen, that they somehow will be set aside because of the righteousness of the Saints, are deceived and will rue the day they harbored such a delusion.

The Lord has warned and forewarned us against a day of great tribulation and given us counsel, through His servants, on how we can be prepared for these difficult times. Have we heeded His counsel?

. . . I bear you my testimony that President Heber J. Grant was inspired of the Lord in establishing the Church Welfare program. The First Presidency was inspired when they made the first public announcement in 1936 and declared the prime purpose of Church welfare was "to help the people help themselves" (in Conference Report, Oct. 1936, p. 3). I bear witness to that inspired counsel from 1936 to the present day that the Saints lay up a year's supply of food. When President Spencer W. Kimball persistently admonishes the members to plant gardens and fruit trees and produce our own food, he is likewise inspired of the Lord.

Be faithful, my brothers and sisters, to this counsel and you will be blessed — yes, the most blessed people in all the earth. You are good people. I know that. But all of us need to be better than we are. Let us be in a position so we are able to not only feed ourselves through the home production and storage, but others as well.

May God bless us to be prepared for the days which lie ahead, which may be the most severe yet.

* * * * * *

Ezra Taft Benson
October Conference, 1987

Fathers, another vital aspect of providing for the material needs of your family is the provision you should be making for your family in case of an emergency. Family preparedness has been a long-established welfare principle. It is even more urgent today. I ask you earnestly, have you provided for your family a year's supply of food, clothing, and, where possible, fuel? The revelation to produce and store food may be as essential to our temporal welfare today as boarding the ark was to the people in the days of Noah.

. . . Yes, brethren, as fathers in Israel you have a great responsibility to provide for the material needs of your family and to have the necessary provisions in case of emergency.

* * * * * *

Ezra Taft Benson
April Conference, 1988

And what about family preparedness? Family preparedness has always been an essential welfare principle in perfecting the Saints. Are each of us and our families following, where permitted, the long-standing counsel to have sufficient food, clothing, and where possible, fuel on hand to last at least one year?

* * * * * *

Victor L. Brown
October Conference, 1975

We realize that it sounds as though these represent some extremes; however, they also represent the facts of life. There are few of us who do not need bolstering in some aspects of personal welfare at some time in our lives.

. . . In the Welfare Services session of conference held last April, Bishop H. Burke Peterson described family preparedness this way: "When we speak of family preparedness, we should speak of foreseen, anticipated, almost expected needs which can be met through wise preparation. Even true emergencies can be modified by good planning." (*Welfare Services Meeting,* April 5, 1975, p. 5.)

Family preparedness is the key to meeting personal welfare needs for the members of the family. Every other aspect of Welfare Services, such as ward preparedness, is designed to support family preparedness.

. . . *Home production and storage.* The prepared family has sufficient stores to take care of basic needs for a minimum of one year. Further, they are, where possible, actively involved in the growing, canning, and sewing, and production of their year's supply.

* * * * * *

Victor L. Brown
April Conference, 1976

A year ago in this Welfare Services meeting, President Marion G. Romney made this comment: "I do not want to be a calamity howler. I don't know in detail what's going to happen in the future. I know what the prophets have predicted. But I tell you that the welfare program, organized to enable us to take care of our own needs, has not yet performed the function that it was set up to perform. We will see the day when we live on what we produce." (*Conference Reports,* April 1975, p. 165.)

President Spencer W. Kimball has said:

"We have had many calamities in this past period. It seems that every day or two there is an earthquake or a flood or a tornado or distress that brings trouble to many people. I am grateful to see that our people and our leaders are beginning to catch the vision of their self-help. . . .

"Now I think the time is coming when there will be more distresses, when there may be more tornadoes, and more floods, . . . more earthquakes. . . . I think they will be increasing probably as we come nearer to the end, and so we must be prepared for this." (*Conference Reports,* April 1974, pp. 183-84.)

* * * * * *

Victor L. Brown
October Conference, 1976

Home production and storage is a very necessary element of personal and family preparedness; however, it is not the only element, nor is it necessarily the most significant element. Some people have reacted to the theme of preparedness as if it were a doomsday matter. In reality, all six elements of personal and family preparedness are to be emphasized so that the Latter-day Saints may be better prepared to meet the ordinary, day-to-day requirements of successful living.

Our emphasis on this subject is not grounds for crisis thinking or panic. Quite the contrary, personal and family preparedness should be a way of provident living, an orderly approach to using the resources, gifts, and talents the Lord shares with us. So the first step is to teach our people to be self-reliant and independent through proper preparation for daily life.

* * * * * *

Victor L. Brown
October Conference, 1978

A couple serving as welfare services missionaries were asked to assist members in planting family gardens. Seeds were obtained by President Castaneda through community resources and distributed to the members. He took the lead by planting the first garden. Almost all of the members followed his example.

It was soon found that in order to raise a garden, provisions had to be made to keep the pigs from running loose. Pens also had to be constructed for the chickens; it seemed that they were able to scratch out the seeds and young plants faster than they could grow.

In addition to the gardens, storage also became a part of the program. Members were taught how to dry fruits and vegetables, and canning was done on a small scale. Jams and jellies were made, using appropriate local methods. Part of their year's supply included grains grown in their fields and then stored. They had to learn how to keep them from being infested by insects and rats. Wood which was brought in from the mountains and stored was later used as fuel for cooking as well as for heating water to wash dishes and clean the house.

As cleanliness and sanitation were emphasized, the members began building bathrooms adjacent to their homes. Prior to the project, members in Bermejillo had no bathrooms.

In this small building [slide shown], the first flush toilet in Bermejillo was installed with a septic tank dug in the courtyard to contain the waste. A shower was also built. It consisted of a fifty-gallon drum on the roof which was filled with water in the morning, warmed by the sun during the day, and was ready for a warm shower in the evening.

. . . Members in Bermejillo had access to water which was piped from a nearby city but which was unsafe to drink. Boiling the water was too difficult because of the scarcity of fuel. So mothers were taught to purify it by putting three drops of chlorine bleach in each quart of water. Purifying the water has reduced illness due to diarrhea, amoebae, and typhoid fever.

* * * * * *

Victor L. Brown
April Conference, 1980

There should be no misunderstanding on this point. The fundamental principle of welfare services is that *you and I provide for our own needs.* If serious economic disruption were to occur, the Church would do all in its power to alleviate suffering by supplementing member efforts. But it would not be able to do for the Saints what we have been taught to do for ourselves for over forty years—that is, to have a year's supply of food, clothing, and, where possible, fuel; to have savings in reserve; and to possess basic production skills. This counsel has been given at least twice a year for all these years. Some have followed the counsel of the Brethren and are prepared, as were the five wise virgins. Some, like the foolish virgins, do not have enough oil in their lamps. (See Matt. 25:1-13.)

A recent Church survey of a representative number of members in the United States indicates that in emergency circumstances—such as job loss, illness, or natural disaster—the average family had the following supplies: food, twenty-six weeks; clothes, fifty-two weeks; water, two weeks; and fuel, four days. This is not even close to a year's supply. The survey also indicates that financial reserves are low. Only 17 percent could live for more than one year on their financial reserves if income were cut off; 45 percent reported they could only live for three months. The Lord says, "If ye are prepared ye shall not fear" (D&C 38:30). I suppose each of us knows into which category he falls. What a wonderful thing it would be if all were prepared.

* * * * * *

Victor L. Brown
October Conference, 1980

I do not want to leave the impression that nothing has been done. There are those faithful Saints who have their year's supply and are taking care of themselves. They know of that peace which comes from being obedient and being prepared. From letters we receive, we know that many other families are planting gardens and working toward their year's supply of food, clothing, and other necessities. Some parents are striving to get the whole family involved in temporal welfare.

. . . We have been taught that we should build our reserves over a period of time, that we should not go into debt to do so, that we should buy those things we use and use them on a rotation basis, that we should use common sense in preparing ourselves to be independent and self-reliant. There has never been extremism or fanaticism associated with these teachings.

. . . Our concern and the thrust of my message, which has been repeated from this pulpit many times, is that the welfare program rests on the basic principle of personal and family preparedness, not on Church preparedness. We are concerned that because the Church program includes production projects, canneries, bishops' storehouses, Deseret Industries, and other visible activities, our people are mistakenly led to believe these things replace the need for them to provide for themselves. This simply is not so.

. . . It would appear that in altogether too many cases the teachings about preparedness have been either misjunderstood or knowingly rejected. Many of our members appear to feel that when difficulty comes, the Church will come to their aid, even when they could have prepared themselves had their priorities been appropriate.

* * * * * *

Victor L. Brown
October Conference, 1980

My brothers and sisters, I feel our anxieties are justified. It is the opinion of many that more dificult times lie ahead. We are deeply concerned about the welfare of our people and recognize the potential privation and suffering that will exist if each person and family does not accept the word of the Lord when he says, "Prepare every needful thing" (D&C 88:119), and "It must needs be done in mine own way" (D&C 104:16).

. . . May I again implore you priesthood and Relief Society leaders to see that all members of the Church everywhere understand the responsibility they have for their own welfare, that our people will be blessed to live provident and righteous lives.

* * * * * *

Victor L. Brown
October Conference, 1982

In 1970, President Harold B. Lee said, "For thirty years the leaders of this church have been telling us to store food and to prepare for a rainy day. We have listened, many have paid no attention, and now suddenly disaster begins to strike and some of those who have been slothful are running to the banks and taking out their savings, and buying . . . foodstuffs." (Welfare agricultural meeting, 4 April 1970.)

* * * * * *

F. Enzio Busche
Ensign, June 1982

Frequently I am asked, "What were the most valuable items in the days of starvation in Germany?"

. . . As for what we needed, the food item we relied on most was vegetable oil. With a bottle of vegetable oil, one could acquire nearly every other desirable item. It had such value that with a quart of vegetable oil one could probably trade for three bushels of apples or three hundred pounds of potatoes. Vegetable oil has a high calorie content, is easy to transport, and in cooking can give a tasty flavor to all kinds of food items that one would not normally consider as food—wild flowers, wild plants, and roots from shrubs and trees. For me and my family, a high-quality vegetable oil has the highest priority in our food storage, both in times of daily use and for emergency usage. When vegetable oil is well-packed and stored appropriately, it has a long storage life without the necessity of refrigeration. We found ours to be in very good condition after twenty years of storage, but circumstances may vary in different countries and with different supplies.

. . . The second highest priority item *for me and my family* is grain in all its form, preferably wheat and rye. When grain is well-packed and well-preserved, it too is easy to transport, easy to store, and will last for generations.

A third priority item is honey. Its value in daily usage is immeasurable. My family prefers honey rather than sugar because our experience supports some of the research findings regarding the preeminence of honey. Another reason I prefer honey is because during the starvation period in postwar Germany, honey could be traded for three times as much as sugar; its value was considered that much greater.

A fourth important food storage product is powdered milk.

These four basic items—oil, wheat, honey, and milk (or their equivalents in other cultures)—together with water, salt, and renewable basic foods such as potatoes and other vegetables, can satisfy nutritional requirements in times of emergency and also are valuable and usable in normal daily life.

You might ask, "What about the many other food items and desserts that play an important role in our eating habits?" I shall always treasure the great experience I had in those hard times, when I learned to appreciate food with the most balanced nutrients. When a person is very hungry, the taste of food will change for him. In times of emergency, the Lord seems to provide a way to help our bodies adapt.

. . . When we think in terms of our own year's supply of those foods and materials we use on a regular basis, we may feel that every family will have to store everything. This, of course, is not easy and seems to make storage difficult. However, let me offer this comforting idea based on past experience. We need to take into consideration that in difficult times, so long as there survives more than one family, there will be trading of valuable items. A free market will begin immediately to satisfy the needs of people, and items in greatest demand will set the price, bypassing the use of money. The ingeniousness of mankind becomes evident in times of need. When man is presented with a problem or challenge, if he is in a healthy spirit — which hopefully we are — he will find solutions that he never dreamed of. When a person has a good, healthy spirit, is able to adjust and is not afraid to use his imagination, he will find ways to survive.

There is a long way from the point of hunger to actual starvation, and there is much that one can do to stay alive in hard times, especially when one is mentally and physically prepared. A garden, even as small as a window box, is of great value, as is the skill to be able to plant and to grow things. Following the war, in addition to having a small garden, my family was able to obtain the milk we needed by keeping a milk sheep, which gave enough milk for our family for the greater part of the year. (I have not seen this species in America, but it was very common in Germany.) Besides milk, our sheep supplied us with wool to trade or to use for knitting items. During the spring of the year it would give birth to one or two lambs which could also be used for food or trade. Some of our neighbors had goats, but we preferred the sheep because of the wool and because sheep seemed easier to tolerate and to work with. They required very little extra care and were easy to satisfy. Also, all over the country, even the large cities, people began to keep rabbits in small pens, and children had the task of looking for grass, dandelions, and leaves in order to feed their rabbits. In addition, people kept hens, and chicken coops were prevalent in all places. Because grain was too valuable to feed to chickens, other sources of chicken feed had to be found. Children found ways of breeding worms, beetles, and flies to be used for this purpose. People also built small, wooden handcarts which could be used to transport items used for trading, which took place wherever people met.

There are some other observations one could also make: The true nature of people becomes obvious in times of real need. Good people become better; they get close to one another; they learn to share and become united. The strength that develops out of unity of the many good people becomes a real survival factor. On the other hand, people who lack emotional stability become cruel and ruthless under trying circumstances; however, they do not seem to become an overbearing threat because of the closeness and unity of the majority of the people. Therefore, strangely enough, those who have survived hardships look back with fond memories to the awful period of pain and destruction because they recall the closeness that developed as they united themselves to survive by sharing whatever they had.

* * * * * *

J. Reuben Clark, Jr.
April Conference, 1937

At the April 1937 general conference of the Church, President J. Reuben Clark, Jr., of the First Presidency, asked: "What may we as a people and as individuals do for ourselves to prepare to meet this oncoming disaster, which God in his wisdom may not turn aside from us?" President Clark then set forth these inspired basic principles of the Church welfare program:

"First, and above and beyond everything else, let us live righteously. . . .

"Let us avoid debt as we would avoid a plague; where we are now in debt, let us get out of debt; if not today, then tomorrow.

"Let us straitly and strictly live within our incomes, and save a little.

"Let every head of every household see to it that he has on hand enough food and clothing, and, where possible, fuel also, for at least a year ahead. You of small means put your money in foodstuffs and wearing apparel, not in stocks and bonds; you of large means will think you know how to care for yourselves, but I may venture to suggest that you do not speculate. Let every head of every household aim to own his own home, free from mortgage. Let every man who has a garden spot, garden it; every man who owns a farm, farm it." (*Conference Report,* April 1937, p. 26.)

* * * * * *

J. Reuben Clark, Jr.
The Deseret News, February 8, 1941

We are approaching troublous times. I have been talking about them for years. They seem to be upon us. We shall have a period — how long I know not — of what we shall call prosperity; and then there will be something else. I have felt from the time this plan was put into operation that what we were really doing here was not alone caring for our people at this time, when there were so many other avenues open for them to get their help, but we were building for future times when we might need all of our experience, all of our training and skill, all of our intelligence to preserve ourselves and those who might be less fortunate among us than we ourselves may personally be.

I for one can visualize a condition, it may or may not come, when the best of us today will be not much better off than the poorest of us are now. I do not want to seem too pessimistic, but the world faces one of the greatest crises in its history, and no mortal man, without the inspiration of the Lord, can tell where it will lead.

* * * * * *

J. Reuben Clark, Jr.
Address delivered to welfare works at the
Grant Ward Chapel, Cottonwood Stake, May 9, 1944

Man is so constituted that he must be either provident or improvident. Sometimes the Latter-day Saints have been criticized, for being provident. Man is what I would call a seasonable animal, by which I mean that his living comes from things that are produced only a part of the year. We produce in the summer, and we consume in the winter. We are like the bees and the squirrels. The improvident hive perishes. The improvident squirrel dies, and the improvident man, except for the help which he gets, perishes.

Now, there is no excuse for calling a man a hoarder because he is provident enough to put away in the summer what he must needs have in the winter; and remember, that has been the thesis that we have talked about during all the time that we have had the welfare plan.

Recently the report came to us that some man had said to his wife, "Well, we have put away food now for several years, something in the summer to keep us in the winter. Nothing has happened. We will try it once more; and then if famine does not come this is the last time. That will prove that the General Authorities did not have any inspiration."

*   *   *   *   *   *

J. Reuben Clark, Jr.
Church News, March 2, 1946

Now there are several classes of unfortunates and I think if I were a bishop at the present moment, facing the problems that seem to lie ahead, there are certain things which I would do. Before developing that, may I say this: If in 1936 we had told the Saints, "You would better prepare, because the time is coming when"—remember, in 1936 the problem was money,—there was always enough to buy, but the problem today is something to buy, not money—if we had told you then that the time would come when you could not buy all the meat you wanted, and perhaps not any at times; that you could not get butter, and that you could not get sugar, and that you could not get clothing, and that the farmers could not get machinery, and so on down the whole list of things that you can not get now, and that therefore you should prepare for a stormy day, we would have been laughed to scorn. But I say to you again, the advice then given is good today, and you would better prepare for the times ahead, that you may not be like the five foolish virgins with no oil in your lamps.

*   *   *   *   *   *

J. Reuben Clark, Jr.
Church News, April 20, 1946

Now I want to say another word. I have said this often. Cash is not food, it is not clothing, it is not coal, it is not shelter, and we have got to the place where no matter how much cash we have, we cannot secure those things in the quantities which we may need. So notwithstanding, you men of affairs, how much money you have in the bank, you cannot buy all the butter you want if you are very much of a butter eater; you cannot get all the meat you want, and so on through the whole list of things. All that you can be certain you will have is that which you produce; and I say again, as I have said before, it will not surprise me, if times get harder and tighter, if somewhere along the line you will be required to give up what you yourselves have or part of it in your cellars. It will be fortunate if you have put away enough so that you can spare some and still be able to live.

*   *   *   *   *   *

J. Reuben Clark, Jr.
Address given at Pioneer Region
Reported in the Church Section,
Deseret News, December 31, 1955

"I do know that if we go forward in this welfare plan and follow the admonitions given, to put something in the cellar store place that we may have against a rainy day, we may be blessed. This welfare plan is the answer to all home supplies . . . if we come into dire times than all the financial plans of the world will have no value. You can't eat money."

*   *   *   *   *   *

President J. Reuben Clark, Jr.
at Welfare Conference, The Assembly Hall
October 11, 1958

"I still have apprehension that we may have hard times. I still fear that we are going to have a war before too long that on each side will be intended to be a virtually exterminating war. I would like each one of you to think of having around you—you farmers—a production that would enable you to live (and possibly for a while without too much mechanization), and help some of your city folk to live, too. It is a terrible picture even to think about, but we will be shortsighted if we do not."

*   *   *   *   *   *

J. Reuben Clark, Jr.
Wasatch Stake Welfare Meeting, 1959

"I regard the welfare plan as a very essential part of the Gospel plan. . . . Church members should store food as well as clothing for at least a year—preferably two.

"We can't eat money—we need food, and we can't buy it if there is none to buy."

* * * * * *

President J. Reuben Clark, Jr.
From *The Improvement Era* Magazine
September 1961, pgs 632-33

(Article "President J. Reuben Clark, Jr.—An Appreciation on His 90th Birthday" by Harold B. Lee.)

We heard him reply in answer to a question as to why he had put his life savings into his presently owned Grantsville ranch; "This is all I have to leave to my family when I die, and if they are not too lazy to work it, they won't starve. I have told them that when the first atomic bomb is dropped here in America, that they are to go out there on the ranch and stay until it is over." This last seemed not only to be wise council, but also a prophecy. His only son, J. Reuben Clark, III, is the family steward of this practical and foresighted legacy.

* * * * * *

J. Richard Clark
October Conference, 1980

My dear brothers and sisters, the greatest test for any generation is how it responds to the voice of the prophets. Our prophets have admonished us to—

1. Increase our personal righteousness.
2. Live within our means and get out of debt.
3. Produce, can, and store enough food, clothing, and, where possible, fuel for one year.

This straightforward counsel has not been followed by all of you. Some have believed and complied; others have waited until they could be sure the storm clouds were really gathering; and still others have rejected the counsel.

. . . *People respond only to what they are prepared to believe.* The Brethren hesitate sometimes to talk in bold terms regarding the realities of the economy and the need for individual and family preparedness. Such talk is interpreted by the black-cloud watchers as a time of general calamity, and many stampede to the grocery stores to get ahead of the hoarders.

In April 1976 Bishop Featherstone suggested a one-year goal for members to store a year's supply of food. Some of those who had not yet begun a home storage program rushed out and plunged deeply into debt to buy hundreds of dollars of groceries. They then sat back, as did the Prophet Jonah, to see what was going to happen to Nineveh: It was as if Brother Featherstone had officially set doomsday as April 1, 1977. This was not his intention. The Lord's way has always been an orderly preparation, not one of second-guessing, confusion, and panic.

. . . Finally, concerning the insufficiency of reserves, God gave a natural instinct to the animals he created to preserve their surplus against a time of need. But man has developed the tendency to squander all that he harvests and to leave to chance or to others his satisfaction of future needs. This is contrary to divine law. Frugality is a principle of righteousness. Consumption should never exceed our production. Economic freedom comes from the surpluses we create.

In addition to our reserve of food, we should build a cash reserve.

* * * * * *

J. Richard Clark
October Conference, 1980

. . . One final concern of reserve deficiency is the need to insure against our greatest potential loss. I think we all would agree that our ability to earn is our greatest asset. When the provider insures his life, he is insuring his future income for his family. As husbands, let us not force our wives into the marketplace to be both the provider and homemaker should our lives be cut short by premature death. We can increase their options by proper insurance planning.

We would also urge each family to carry adequate health insurance. Medical costs are soaring, and trying to self-insure from personal savings is very risky. During inflation, medical costs increase faster than our savings accumulate.

. . . There are some who feel that they are secure as long as they have funds to purchase food. Money is not food. If there is no food in the stores or in the warehouses, you cannot sustain life with money. Both President Romney and President Clark have warned us that we will yet live on what we produce.

. . . I would like to make one point very clear. The welfare services program of the Church is essentially you and I being self-sufficient within our own families. The Church storehouse system is a backup system for the small number of members who are poor or physically handicapped, or for emergencies or disasters. There is *no way* the Church, as an institution, intends to assume the responsibility that rightfully belongs to the individual. The welfare program was never designed to do so. Personal and family preparedness is the Lord's way. Then, by uniting together to pay generous fast offerings and by providing commodities from our projects and canneries, we can help our neighbor who cannot help himself.

Most important of all, brothers and sisters, with all our storing, let us store righteousness that we may stand approved of the Lord.

* * * * * *

Matthew Cowley
Matthew Cowley Speaks
Deseret Book, 1954

There is something in the Doctrine and Covenants, which says, "And there shall be a great hailstorm sent forth to destroy the crops of the earth." (D&C 29:16). . . . What are you going to do when that happens? Ah, brothers and sisters, [support] your welfare project, and when that happens and if you have your year's supply of food in your home, let the hails come, and the winds blow, and our storehouses in our homes, in our wards, and in our stakes will be full just as they were in the days of Joseph, and we will be preserved.

I like that plan. What good will be our greenbacks that we get from the government for security when all the crops of the earth are destroyed by hail? . . . You know in the days of Israel they worked this plan.

* * * * * *

James E. Faust
April Conference, 1986

President Spencer W. Kimball counseled: "I hope that we understand that, while having a garden, for instance, is often useful in reducing food costs and making available delicious fresh fruits and vegetables, it does much more than this. Who can gauge the value of that special chat between daughter and Dad as they weed or water the garden? How do we evaluate the good that comes from the obvious lessons of planting, cultivating, and the eternal law of the harvest? And how do we measure the family togetherness and cooperating that must accompany successful canning? Yes, we are laying up resources in store, but perhaps the greater good is contained in the lessons of life we learn as we live providently and extend to our children their pioneer heritage." (In Conference Report, Oct. 1977, p. 125; *Ensign*, Nov. 1977, p. 78.) This heritage includes teaching our children how to work.

. . . The counsel to have a year's supply of basic food, clothing, and commodities was given fifty years ago and has been repeated many times since. Every father and mother are the family's storekeepers. They should store whatever their own family would like to have in the case of an emergency. Most of us cannot afford to store a year's supply of luxury items, but find it more practical to store staples that might keep us from starving in case of emergency. Surely we all hope that the hour of need will never come. Some have said, "We have followed this counsel in the past and have never had need to use our year's supply, so we have difficulty keeping this in mind as a major priority." Perhaps following this counsel could be the reason why they have not needed to use their reserve. By continued rotation of the supply it can be kept usable with no waste.

The Church cannot be expected to provide for every one of its millions of members in case of public or personal disaster. It is therefore necessary that each home and family do what they can to assume the responsibility for their own hour of need. If we do not have the resources to acquire a year's supply, then we can strive to begin with having one month's supply. I believe if we are provident and wise in the management of our personal and family affairs and are faithful, God will sustain us through our trials. He has revealed: "For the earth is full, and there is enough and to spare; yea, I prepared all things, and have given unto the children of men to be agents unto themselves." (D&C 104:17.)

* * * * * *

James E. Faust
April Conference, 1986

The old couplet "Waste not, want not" still has much merit. Frugality requires that we live within our income and save a little for a rainy day, which always seems to come.

* * * * * *

Vaughn J. Featherstone
April Conference, 1976

For twenty-six years, since I was fifteen, I was involved in the grocery industry. I learned much about human nature during those years. I remember the effects that strikes, earthquakes, and rumors of war had on many very active Latter-day Saints. Like the five foolish virgins, they rushed to the store to buy food, caught in the panic of knowing that direction had been given by the prophet but not having followed that direction—fearful that maybe they had procrastinated until it was everlastingly too late.

It was interesting because only in Latter-day Saint communities did people seem to buy with abandon. It was not a few Latter-day Saints—it was a significant number. It caused great increases in sales. One such experience came when a so-called prophecy by someone outside the Church was greatly publicized.

How foolish we can sometimes be! We having a living prophet; we have God's living oracles, the First Presidency and the Council of the Twelve Apostles. Let us follow the Brethren and be constant. We need have no fear if we are prepared.

. . . Brothers and sisters, what have we done in our stakes and wards to see that every Latter-day Saint has a year's reserve of food to sustain life? Let's not only keep teaching the principle, but let's also teach our people how.

. . . Second, decide what is needed to bring your present reserve levels to a year's supply. Then make a list and prepare a plan. Consider first, what are the basics? —wheat (or grain from your locale), sugar or honey, dried milk, salt, and water. Most of us can afford such basics. Buy them from your monthly food budget allowance. The Church discourages going into debt to buy for storage.

Now that you know where you are and where you need to be, the third step is to work out a time schedule for when you will reach your goal. I suggest that one year from today we ought to have a year's supply of food in all active—and many inactive—members' homes in the Church. Where food storage violates the law of your land, then abide the law. However, even in those cases we can plant gardens and fruit trees and raise rabbits or chickens. Do all you can within the laws of your community, and the Lord will bless you when the time of need comes. Now here are some suggestions how:

1. Follow the prophet. He has counseled us to plant a garden and fruit trees. This year don't just think about it—do it. Grow all the food you possibly can. Also remember to buy a year's supply of garden seeds so that, in case of a shortage, you will have them for the following spring. I'm going to tell you where to get the money for all the things I'm going to suggest.

2. Find someone who sells large bulk of grains, depending on your locale. Make arrangements to buy a ton or so of grain.

3. Find someone who sells honey in large containers and make arrangements to buy what you can afford on a regular basis or buy a little additional sugar each time you go to the store.

4. Purchase dry milk from the store or dairy, on a systematic basis.

5. Buy a case of salt the next time you go to the store. In most areas, 24 one-pound packages will cost you less than $5.

6. Store enough water for each member of your family to last for at least two weeks.

Where the foods I mentioned are not available or are not basic in your culture or area, make appropriate substitutions.

. . . Now you ask, "Where do I get the money for these things? I agree we need them, but I'm having a hard time making ends meet."

Here is how you do it. Use any one or all of these suggestions, some of which may not be applicable in your country:

1. Decide as a family this year that 25 or 50 percent of your Christmas will be spent on a year's supply. Many families in the Church spend considerable sums of money for Christmas. Half or part of these Christmas monies will go a long way toward purchasing the basics. Brethren, give your wife a year's supply of wheat for Christmas, and she'll know your heart is in the right place.

2. When you desire new clothes, don't buy them. Repair and mend and make your present wardrobe last a few months longer. Use that money for the food

basics. Make all of your nonfood necessities that you feasibly can, such as furniture and clothing.

3. Cut the amount of money you spend on recreation by 50 percent. Do fun things that do not require money outlay but make more lasting impressions on your children.

4. Decide as a family that there will be no vacation or holiday next year unless you have your year's supply. Many Church members could buy a full year's supply of the basics from what they would save by not taking a vacation. Take the vacation time and work on a family garden. Be together, and it can be just as much fun.

5. If you haven't a year's supply yet and you do have boats, snowmobiles, campers, or other luxury possessions, sell or trade one or two or more of them and get your year's supply.

6. Watch advertised specials in the grocery stores and pick up extra supplies of those items that are of exceptional value.

7. Change the mix in your family's diet. Get your protein from sources less expensive than meat. The grocery bill is one bill that can be cut. Every time you enter the store and feel tempted by effective and honest merchandising to buy cookies, candy, ice cream, nonfood items, or magazines—don't! Think carefully; buy only the essentials. Then figure what you have saved and spend it on powdered milk, sugar, honey, salt, or grain.

. . . The Lord will make it possible, if we make a firm commitment, for every Latter-day Saint family to have a year's supply of food reserves by April 1977. All we have to do is to decide, commit to do it, and then keep the commitment. Miracles will take place; the way will be opened, and next April we will have our storage areas filled. We will prove through our actions our willingness to follow our beloved prophet and the Brethren, which will bring security to us and our families.

. . . Now regarding home production: Raise animals where means and local laws permit. Plant fruit trees, grapevines, berry bushes, and vegetables. You will provide food for your family, much of which can be eaten fresh. Other food you grow can be preserved and included as part of your home storage. Wherever possible, produce your nonfood necessities of life. Sew and mend your own clothing. Make or build needed items. I might also add, beautify, repair, and maintain all of your property.

Home production of food and nonfood items is a way to stretch your income and to increase your skills and talents. It is a way to teach your family to be self-sufficient. Our children are provided with much needed opportunities to learn the fundamentals of work, industry, and thrift. President Romney has said, "We will see the day when we will live on what we produce." (*Conference Reports,* April 1975, p. 165.)

. . . I should like to address a few remarks to those who ask, "Do I share with my neighbors who have not followed the counsel? And what about the nonmembers who do not have a year's supply? Do we have to share with them?" No, we don't *have* to share—we *get* to share! Let us not be concerned about silly thoughts of whether we would share or not. Of course we would share! What would Jesus do? I could not possibly eat food and see my neighbors starving. And if you starve to death after sharing, "greater love hath no man than this. . ." (John 15:13.)

Now what about those who would plunder and break in and take that which we have stored for our families' needs? Don't give this one more idle thought. There is a God in heaven whom we have obeyed. Do you suppose he would abandon those who have kept his commandments? He said, "If ye are prepared, ye need not fear." (D&C 38:30.) Prepare, O men of Zion, and fear not. Let Zion put on her beautiful garments. Let us put on the full armor of God. Let us be pure in heart, love mercy, be just, and stand in holy places. Commit to have a year's supply of food by April 1977.

. . . In his October 1973 conference address, President Ezra Taft Benson gave some excellent instructions about home storage:

"For the righteous the gospel provides a warning before a calamity, a program for the crises, a refuge for each disaster. . . .

"The Lord has warned us of famines, but the righteous will have listened to prophets and stored at least a year's supply of survival food. . . .

"Brethren and sisters, I know that this welfare program is inspired of God. I have witnessed with my own eyes the ravages of hunger and destitution as, under the direction of the president of the Church, I spent a year in war-torn Europe at the close of World War II, without my family, distributing food, clothing, and bedding to our needy members. I have looked into the sunken eyes of Saints, in almost the last stages of starvation. I have seen faithful mothers carrying their children, three and four years of age, who were unable to walk because of malnutrition. I have seen a hungry woman turn down food for a spool of thread. I have seen grown men weep as they ran their hands through the wheat and beans sent to them from Zion—America.

"Thanks be to God for a prophet, for this inspired program, and for Saints who so managed their stewardship that they could provide for their own and still share with others." ("Prepare Ye," *Ensign*, Jan. 1974, pp. 69, 81-82.)

. . . I bear my humble witness to you that the great God of heaven will open doors and means in a way we never would have supposed to help all those who truly want to get their year's supply. I know we will have time and money if we will commit and keep the commitment.

* * * * * *

J. Thomas Fyans
October Conference, 1979

The real strength of the Church lies in the savings accounts, the gardens, the income-producing skills, the home storage, the resiliency, the talents, and the testimonies of each individual member of the Church and in the family of which each of us is a part. Let us be ever mindful that the greatest blessing of the welfare system is derived by the givers and that each of us should work to be independent and self-reliant as families in order to be in a position to help our less fortunate brothers and sisters. Stated in plainness, each family unit's *personal and family preparedness activity* is every bit as important as this vast and marvelous welfare system. The real strength of the Church does not ultimately lie in the financial and commodity reserves of the Church; rather, it rests in the reserves and strength of every household. May I illustrate.

Suppose for a moment that the four million plus members of the Church lived in an area approximately the size of the state of Utah. And suppose that we were worried about wild, ferocious animals coming into the land in which we lived. The streets would be unsafe, so we would decide to build a wall to protect us. Now, if we took the total reserves stored in all our Church storehouses and used these goods to build an encircling wall around this area, it would be one foot wide by one foot high stretching some twelve hundred miles. This one-foot-high wall would not deter many animals from entering our area of hoped-for safety.

Now, let us suppose that we would add to that one-foot-high wall the storage that the members of the Church would have if they were to have a year's supply. We could then raise the wall another foot around this area the size of the state of Utah. And then another foot, and then another foot, and then another foot, and then another foot, and then another foot until we would have a wall over fourteen feet high.

. . . You see, our total protection cannot come solely from the production of the welfare projects of the Church. It will come only as we combine with that production our individual family's year's supply.

* * * * * *

Gordon B. Hinkley
Ensign, July 1984

I am profoundly grateful for the essence of that spirit of helpfulness which has come down through the generations and which has been so evident in the troubles Latter-day Saints experience in time of disaster and difficulty. The mayor of Salt Lake City told me that when the Salt Lake City flood situation became serious one Sunday afternoon in 1983 that he called a stake president. Within a very short time 4,000 volunteers showed up. The story of such mutual helpfulness caught the attention of many individuals and publications across the nation. Latter-day Saints, working together with their neighbors of other faiths, have labored with one another in times of distress and have been heralded on radio and television, in newspapers and magazines. Writers have treated it as if it were a new and unique phenomenon.

* * * * * *

President Gordon B. Hinkley
October Conference, 1985

"What about the arms race, and particularly the nuclear arms buildup?"

"Again it is a sad commentary on our civilization that the peace of the world hangs on a balance of terror. No one understanding the facts can doubt that a rash decision could lead to the extermination of the race. It is to be hoped that representatives of the great powers will continue to talk and will seek with sincere and earnest desire to find ways to ameliorate the terrible threat which hangs over the world. I am of the opinion that if a catastrophe is to be avoided, there must be widely cultivated a strong and compelling will for peace on the part of men and women in all nations. Let us, who are followers of the Prince of Peace, pray with great faith, in His name, that the world may be spared a consuming catastrophe that could come from some misadventure."

* * * * * *

Orson Hyde
Quoted by Ezra Taft Benson
October Conference, 1980

There is more salvation and security in wheat than in all the political schemes of the world.

* * * * * *

Spencer W. Kimball
Funeral Sermon, Arizona, 1943

Though food be scarce, and starvation stalks abroad, men will still share their portion, give succor to the afflicted, sympathy to the bereaved, and help to the unfortunate. Though cities be bombed, families separated, the meaning of sympathy and understanding and brotherhood will not change. Courage is not dead, ambition is not slain, love is not replaced. The bombed cities shall rise again, the grain that was burned shall be replanted, the fountain that evil has polluted shall flow pure again, the battered forests will shoot forth new foliage and the grass will spring forth anew to obliterate the traces of war. Even though a thousand times they shall afflict the earth, a thousand times will it come forth again and men will survive to plant the ground and build upon it. The conditions of life in this chaotic situation are changed, but the meaning of the fundamentals of life have not changed.

* * * * * *

Spencer W. Kimball
General Conference, *Improvement Era,* June 1960

Men depend on armaments as on idols. O foolish men who think to protect the world with armaments, battleships, and space equipment, when only righteousness is needed!

The answer to all of our problems—personal, national, and international—has been given to us many times by many prophets, ancient and modern. Why must we grovel in the earth when we could be climbing toward heaven! The path is not obscure. Perhaps it is too simple for us to see. We look to foreign programs, summit conferences, land bases. We depend on fortifications, or gods of stone; upon ships and planes and projectiles, our gods of iron—gods which have no ears, no eyes, no hearts. We pray to them for deliverance and depend upon them for protection . . . like the gods of Baal.

* * * * * *

Spencer W. Kimball
General Conference, *Improvement Era,* December 1961

While the iron curtains rise and thicken, we eat, drink, and make merry. While armies are marshalled and march and drill, and officers teach men how to kill, we continue to drink and carouse as usual. While bombs are detonated and tested, and fallout settles on the already sick world, we continue in idolatry and adultery. While corridors are threatened and concessions made, we live riotously and divorce and marry in cycles like the seasons. While leaders quarrel, and editors write, and authorities analyze and prognosticate, we break the Sabbath as though no command had ever been given. While enemies filter into our nation to subvert us and intimidate us and soften us, we continue with our destructive thinking: "It can't happen here."

Will we ever turn wholly to God? Fear envelopes the world which could be at ease and peace. In God is protection, safety, peace. He has said, "I will fight your battles." But his commitment is on condition of our faithfulness.

* * * * * *

Spencer W. Kimball
"Who Contendeth with the Almighty"
Prepared for Area Conferences in Manchester, England but not delivered, August 1971

Maintain a year's supply. The Lord has urged that his people save for the rainy days, prepare for the difficult times, and put away for emergencies, a year's supply or more of bare necessities so that when comes the flood, the earthquake, the famine, the hurricane, the storms of life, our families can be sustained through the dark days. How many of us have complied with this? We strive with the Lord, finding many excuses: We do not have room for storage. The food spoils. We do not have the funds to do it. We do not like these common foods. It is not needed—there will always be someone to help in trouble. The government will come to the resuce. And some intend to obey but procrastinate.

* * * * * *

Spencer W. Kimball
Welfare Services Meeting, April 6, 1974

We have had many calamities in this past period. It seems that every day or two there is an earthquake or a flood or a tornado or distress that brings trouble to many people. I am grateful to see that our people and our leaders are beginning to catch the vision of their self-help.

Let me say that as a stake president long ago, we had a flood in the Duncan Valley in Arizona. As soon as we overcame the excitement of the first report of it, my counselors and I formulated a telegram and sent it to Salt Lake City and said, "Please send us $10,000 by return mail." I found that I was learning about welfare programs when no $10,000 came. When President Lee, President Romney and President Moyle came down and

took me back in my little office in my business place we sat down around the table and they said, "This isn't a program of 'give me.' This is a program of 'self-help.'" And so we learned much from those brethren.

. . . Something was said about gardens and about trees. I should say that in our little yard Sister Kimball is our farmer, and she nearly feeds us through the year from that little yard in the back. We have carrots, and we have apricots, and we have applesauce, and we have other things that help. Then she plants beans along the grillwork of our back porch, down among the roses, and they climb up over all this grillwork. I joke with her a lot of times about having done that so she can sit in her rocking chair and pick the beans, but we just almost live on beans and it is good food, very good food. The little gardens and the few trees are very valuable. I remember when the sisters used to say, "Well, but we could buy it at the store a lot cheaper than we can put it up." But that isn't quite the answer, is it, Sister Spafford? Because there will come a time when there isn't a store. I remember long years ago that I asked a very prominent grocer who had a chain of grocery stores, "How long would your supply of groceries last if you did not have trucks to bring in new supplies?" And he said, "Maybe we could stretch it out two weeks from our storehouses and from our supplies." People could get awfully hungry after two weeks were over.

* * * * * *

Spencer W. Kimball
October Conference, 1974

We are also concerned with the great waste from our homes and stores and restaurants and otherwise. After the usual banquet, enough is carried out in the garbage to feed numerous mouths that have been drooling for a bite to eat in less-favored countries. Many are starving, and we throw away much and waste much.

* * * * * *

Spencer W. Kimball
October Conference, 1974

Gardens promote independence. Should evil times come, many might wish they had filled all their fruit bottles and cultivated a garden in their backyards and planted a few fruit trees and berry bushes and provided for their own commodity needs.

The Lord planned that we would be independent of every creature, but we note even many farmers buy their milk from dairies and homeowners buy their garden vegetables from the store. And should the trucks fail to fill the shelves of the stores, many would go hungry.

* * * * * *

Spencer W. Kimball
April Conference, 1976

There are many people in the Church today who have failed to do, and continue to argue against doing, the things that are requested and suggested by this great organization.

The Lord said also, "Not every one that saith unto me, Lord, Lord, shall enter into the kingdom of heaven; but he that doeth the will of my Father which is in heaven." (Matt. 7:21.) And I was thinking that there are as many wards and branches in the Church as there are people in this room, one for one. And what great accomplishment there would be if every bishop and every branch president in all the wold, wherever it's possible (of course there are a few places where this is not permitted), had a storage such as has been suggested here this morning—and took to their three or four or five hundred members the same message, quoting scripture and insisting that the people of their wards and branches do the things the Lord has requested, for we know that there are many who are failing.

And then I hear them argue, "Well, suppose we do put away a lot and then someone comes and takes it from us, our neighbors who do not believe." That's been answered this morning.

. . . Think of the number of people represented here this day by the stake presidents, mission presidents, and others who are directors, who have many people under them. Our 750 stakes—all of them including hundreds, could show the power that we have, if we go to work and actually push this matter until it is done. We talk about it, we listen to it, but sometimes we do not *do* the things which the Lord says.

Brethren and sisters, we've gathered here this morning to consider the important program which we must never forget nor put in the background. As we become more affluent and our bank accounts enlarge, there comes a feeling of security, and we feel sometimes that we do not need the supply that has been suggested by the Brethren. It lies there and deteriorates, we say. And suppose it does? We can reestablish it. We must remember that conditions could change and a year's supply of basic commodities could be very much appreciated by us or others. So we would do well to listen to what we have been told and to follow it explicitly.

. . . There are some countries which prohibit savings or surpluses. We do not understand it, but it is true. And we honor, obey, and sustain the laws of the country which is ours. (See Twelfth Article of Faith.) Where it is permitted, though, which is most of the world, we should listen to the counsel of the Brethren and to the Lord.

Recognizing that the family is the basic unit of both the Church and society generally, we call upon Latter-day Saints everywhere to strengthen and beautify the home with renewed effort in these specific areas: food production, preservation, storage; the production and storage of nonfood items; fixup and cleanup of homes and surroundings. We wish to say another word about this in the next meeting.

We encourage you to grow all the food that you feasibly can on your own property. Berry bushes, grapevines, fruit trees—plant them if your climate is right for their growth. Grow vegetables and eat them from your own yards. Even those residing in apartments or condominiums can generally grow a little food in pots and planters. Study the best methods of providing your own foods. Make your garden as neat and attractive as well as productive. If there are children in your home, involve them in the process with assigned responsibilities.

. . . Avoid debt. We used to talk about that a great deal, but today everything is seemingly geared toward debt. "Get your cards, and buy everything on time": you're encouraged to do it. But the truth is that we *don't* need to do it to live.

From local sources seek out reliable information on food and nonfood preservation. If additional information is needed, priesthood and Relief Society leaders may write, "Home Production and Storage," 50 East North Temple Street, Salt Lake City, Utah 84150, and get all the information you need. We encourage all Latter-day Saint families to become self-reliant and independent.

. . . "But if any provide not for his own, and specially for those of his own house, he hath denied the faith, and is worse [worse!] than an infidel." (1 Tim. 5:8.)

. . . Develop your skills in your home preservation and storage. We reaffirm the previous counsel the Church has always given, to acquire and maintain a year's supply—a year's supply of the basic commodities for us. And Brother Featherstone has pretty well outlined those commodities for us.

Wherever possible, produce your nonfood necessities of life. Improve your sewing skills; sew and mend clothing for your family. All the girls want to learn to type, they all want to go to an office. They don't seem to want to sew anymore, and to plant and protect and renew the things that they use. Develop handicraft skills as the sisters have told us, and make or build needed items.

. . . I've always felt to commend the sisters who tat and knit and crochet, who always have something new and sparkling about the place. We've always been pleased when we've found young women who could make their own clothes and sew well and cook meals and keep the house tidy.

. . . We encourage families to have on hand this year's supply; and we say it over and over and over and repeat over and over the scripture of the Lord where He says, "Why call ye me, Lord, Lord, and do not the things which I say?" How empty it is as they put their spirituality, so-called, into action and call him by his important names, but fail to do the things which he says.

. . . God bless us that we may have the determination to carry forward all of these commandments of the Lord which have been conveyed to us.

* * * * * *

Spencer W. Kimball
April Conference, 1976

We are most grateful for the excellent response by the people of the Church to our urging that gardens be planted and that fruit trees be cultivated and our places cleaned up and made more livable. We fully endorse the program of Governor Calvin Rampton in Salt Lake City calling for the planting of a million trees for a million people.

From Parowan, Utah, we read this:

"In laying out the town a century ago, each family had room for a garden and some fruit trees in back of their house. Some very fine orchards and gardens were in the public square, even down to the late Nineties. I well remember the fine watermelons they used to produce."

President Tanner and I visited a Canadian community, and on a certain street as far as we could see were homes with beautiful gardens. It was wonderful, and they were varied, and the products of those gardens were most delicious.

Everywhere we go we see backyards with beautiful gardens, a few rows of corn, some carrots, potatoes, onions, squash. In some places flower gardens have been turned into vegetable gardens, or they have shared the space.

Another commendable thing about gardening is the exchange of products by neighbors and the fostering of fellowship and neighborliness.

Another family wrote, "Our old rickety barn is down and a beautiful garden is in its place. Had we realized how proud it would make us to have a beautiful garden where the old, fallen barn stood, we should have made the change long ago."

From another member in a rural area comes this: "The old, leaning, half-fallen barn is attractive now. It is repaired, newly painted. We are very proud of it and hope you will drive by and see the improvement."

Another party writes, "We live in a large forest area. I got my boss to go in with me, and we rented a large vacant lot not far away that had no trees. We had it plowed, disked, fertilized, and did we ever have a garden!"

In the *National Geographic* magazine last month, we clipped a picture of a woman bringing bottled and canned fruit to her storage room, which was full of the products of her labors and was neat and tidy. That's the way the Lord planned that we should prepare and eat our vegetables.

On the whole, we are very proud of the success. We learned that 51 percent of the households in the United States plan a garden for this year, 1976; and there will be plenty of lids and canning jars this season. The garden fever has attacked many people.

Tomatoes appear to be the most popular vegetable, followed by leaf lettuce and squash.

The garden is not only for the saving of funds but for the satisfying of a hobby desire.

It is estimated that some 35 million home vegetable gardens in 1976 will be an increase of 2.5 million over last year, and that about 41 percent of all American households will do some home canning this year. That is more than other years. We commend to you the garden fever.

If every family had a garden and rural families had a cow and chickens, some fruit trees, and a garden, it is amazing how nearly the family could be fed from their own lot.

* * * * * *

Spencer W. Kimball
Ensign, June 1976

Warlike peoples pervert patriotism. We are a warlike people, easily distracted from our assignment of preparing for the coming of the Lord. When enemies rise up, we commit vast resources to the fabrication of gods of stone and steel—ships, planes, missiles, fortifications—and depend on them for protection and deliverance. When threatened, we become antienemy instead of pro-kingdom of God; we train a man in the art of war and call him a patriot, thus, in the manner of Satan's counterfeit of true patriotism, perverting the Savior's teaching:

"Love your enemies, bless them that curse you, do good to them that hate you, and pray for them which despitefully use you, and persecute you;

"That ye may be the children of your Father which is in heaven." (Matthew 5:44-45.)

We forget that if we are righteous the Lord will either not suffer our enemies to come upon us—and this is the special promise to the inhabitants of the land of the Americas—or he will fight our battles for us. . . .

What are we to fear when the Lord is with us? Can we not take the Lord at his word and exercise a particle of faith in him?

* * * * * *

Spencer W. Kimball
Rotary Club, Salt Lake City, June 8, 1976

Preservation of freedom requires effort. Now that Independence Day is here, let us glory in its blessings. It is a strange thing when you stop to think about it. The road to this land of the United States is pretty nearly a one-way street. Everyone wants to come here. Nobody wants to leave. You probably never knew anyone who wanted to give up his American citizenship.

Why is this so? Is it because we have more to eat? Better homes? Better living conditions? That cannot be, because people wanted to come here when this was a country of hardship.

No, it is not just dollars. The early pioneers could have told you what it was. It is freedom. It is personal liberty. It is all of the human rights that millions of Americans have died for.

The sad part of it is that a lot of us take our civil rights for granted. We were born in a free country. We think freedom could never end. But it could. It is ending today in many countries. We could lose it, too.

* * * * * *

Spencer W. Kimball
Special Conference, Rexburg, Idaho
June 13, 1976

Help nonmembers in disaster. Amid all the confusion and disorder [after the Teton Dam disaster], let us be orderly and courteous. Make no distinction between member and nonmember. We have heard inspiring reports of the Christian brotherhood in action. Preserve these good feelings in the challenging weeks ahead. Do not let jealousy or rivalry creep in. Act as the Savior himself would act in the weeks and months of future rebuilding.

* * * * * *

Spencer W. Kimball
Dortmund, West Germany Area Conference
August 8, 1976

Do all of you people have a year's supply of the basic commodities? Be sure that you consider it very seriously. We realize that there may be some situations where it may be difficult, but we want you to keep it in mind. When distress or disaster comes to any of our people, we must be ready to help each other. The Church has storage in many places, and as a Church it can do a great deal to help many people.

* * * * * *

Spencer W. Kimball
Scandinavian Area Conference
Copenhagen, Denmark, August 1976

Now you probably have read of the terrible disaster in Idaho since our last conference. Brother Packer and I visited the scene of the disaster. A big dam burst and flooded many communities. The water that reached as high as twenty or thirty feet deep swished through the homes and the farms and the Church buildings and wreaked great damage. Thousands of head of cattle and other animals were destroyed. We were grateful that the warning came in the daytime when all people could be warned. I think only seven people lost their lives, but the destruction was terrible. We just mention that so that you will be prepared in this area. There are famines and dry periods. There are earthquakes and cyclones and divers problems that arise in the various parts of the country. The thing that pleased us was that our people were partly ready. Even though their own personal supplies were washed away, yet we had a surplus in our storehouses. And almost as soon as the word went out, our trucks were moving to Idaho filled with tons of relief commodities. Ricks College, which was just above the water line, was used for homes and for the feeding of the people. Beds were made all through the college, and tens of thousands of people were taken care of. I suppose hundreds of thousands of meals were supplied.

When we visited the President of the United States recently, I told him, "We are prepared." The Lord said, "If ye are prepared ye shall not fear." (D&C 38:30.) Our Relief Society organizations and our bishoprics and our stake presidents all knew what to do. And the work went forward immediately while the nation was trying to get together and plan and organize.

We want you to be ready with your personal storehouses filled with at least a year's supply. You don't argue why it cannot be done; you just plan to organize and get it done.

* * * * * *

Spencer W. Kimball
Amsterdam Area Conference, August 1976

Elder Packer spoke to us in Copenhagen about a warning. The recent flood in Idaho, caused by the breaking of a great dam, overflowed many LDS communities. But the dam broke on a Saturday morning, so it gave an opportunity to get the warning out. Men rushed to their telephones and called all the people they could think of. The people rushed from their homes, leaving everything, and went to Ricks College, where they were housed and fed for many days because their homes were washed away and all their supplies were destroyed. But because they were warned early, most of the people were saved. Only six people were destroyed, and they were generally people who did not heed the warning. For instance, one older couple said they weren't going to move out of their home. They had a car that they could have gotten out with; but when the floods subsided, they were found drowned in their car. After it was too late and the flood was upon them, they tried to get out; but they were drowned. That is true of numerous youth and others if they will not listen to the warnings. And that is why we are here—to bring the warning message to all the people.

* * * * * *

Spencer W. Kimball
October 1976 Regional Representatives
Seminar Address

Preparedness, when properly pursued, is a way of life, not a sudden, spectacular program.

* * * * * *

Spencer W. Kimball
October Conference, 1976

Our pride is great in the people who have listened and who have planted gardens and orchards and trees in the past months. From all directions we hear of gardens which have made an outstanding contribution. A couple in Alabama wrote, "We had vegetables all during the year. We feel it saved us quite a bit of money."

One authority estimates there will be about 35 million home vegetable gardens this year, up from about 32.5 million last year, and he says that probably 41 percent of all American households will do some home canning this year, as against 37 percent a year ago. Many of the numerous gardens are found in hanging baskets, in containers on stairways, on trellises, and in window boxes.

In Oklahoma a state university makes 240 plots available to married students. In Long Island some 400 plots have been turned over to residents. In Pennsylvania some 200,000 plots were under cultivation.

One authority says, "I have my own garden and have found it's my sanity away from work."

We would add to the garden-orchard project the clearing of yards and homes. We have mentioned it before. Still there are numerous homes with broken-down fences and barns, outbuildings that could probably be torn down or rebuilt, ditch banks that could be cleared. We congratulate all who have listened and followed counsel.

From Frankfurt, Germany, this comes:

"We are two families in the Frankfurt Mission, and we tell you about our garden.

"It was not very easy to find a piece of land in a large city like Frankfurt—it is a tiny garden—and when we rented it, it looked like a wilderness, with a broken fence, a broken cottage, and wild grass all over. It did not discourage us.

"First we made a new fence, repaired the cottage, and digged the whole garden. In the springtime we planted vegetables and the neighbours told us that it would not grow. There is a little stream where we can go on our bikes hanged with cans, and this way we carry our water. We prayed to the Lord that he would bless our garden. The Lord did answer our prayers. Every kind of vegetable came. It is so wonderful to see the plants grow. We take turns now to go to our garden and water our plants. We are happy to have a garden."

. . . We express our affection and sympathy to all those who have suffered in great calamities in the past months. The flood caused by the breaking of the Teton Dam brought misery and loss and suffering to numerous of our good people. With its high wall of water, the flood took nearly everything before it. We are grateful that Ricks College facilities were just above the flood line and served to make a home away from home for many who had lost their homes and to furnish hundreds of thousands of meals during their dilemma. We are very proud indeed of the organization, the faithful work, the hospitality, and the self-sacrifice of numerous helpers in this great tragedy.

Our sympathies go out also to the flood victims in the Big Thompson river flood in Colorado, with all the loss and devastation it brought.

We have deep sympathy for those who suffered loss in the Indonesian earthquake, and the earthquake and tidal wave in the Philippine Islands, and the Guatemala earthquake. We have followed with greatest sympathy and affection all these catastrophic experiences and pray the Lord will bless and sustain those who have suffered.

. . . Also, my father was very responsive. He found that President Layton, who was beginning to get rather old and feeble, didn't have the help to do the things he needed to do, and he had a big orchard. So Father gathered all of us children up, with all the buckets and pans, and with the consent and approval of President Layton we all went down to his orchard and picked fruit on shares. There was a large family of the Laytons and there was a large family of us. We divided the pickings from the orchard and went forward with our program. My dear mother knew how to make ends meet. We had a pantry and that pantry was always filled with bottled fruits and everything else you could think of that was available at the time.

* * * * * *

Spencer W. Kimball
April Conference, 1977

The Lord goes further and says:

"I will . . . destroy your cattle, and make you few in number; and your highways shall be desolate." (Lev. 26:22.)

Can you think how the highways could be made desolate? When fuel and power are limited, when there is none to use, when men will walk instead of ride?

Have you ever thought, my good folks, that the matter of peace is in the hands of the Lord who says:

"And I will bring a sword upon you. . ." (Lev. 26:25.)

Would that be difficult? Do you read the papers? Are you acquainted with the hatreds in the world? What guarantee have you for permanent peace?

". . . and ye shall be delivered into the hand of the enemy." (Lev. 26:25.)

Are there enemies who could and would afflict us? Have you thought of that?

"And I will make your cities waste," he says, "and bring your sanctuaries unto desolation. . . .

"Then shall the land enjoy her sabbaths, as long as it lieth desolate, and ye be in your enemies' land; even then shall the land rest, and enjoy her sabbaths.

"As long as it lieth desolate it shall rest; because it did not rest [when it could] in your sabbaths, when ye dwelt upon it." (Lev. 26:31, 34-35.)

Those are difficult and very serious situations, but they are possible.

. . . The Lord uses the weather sometimes to discipline his people for the violation of his laws.

. . . We deal with many things which are thought to be not so spiritual; but all things are spiritual with the Lord, and he expects us to listen, and to obey, and to follow the commandments.

*   *   *   *   *   *

Spencer W. Kimball
October Conference, 1977

As you know, in the recent past we have placed considerable emphasis on personal and family preparedness. I hope that each member of the Church is responding appropriately to this direction. I also hope that we are understanding and accentuating the positive and not the negative.

I like the way the Relief Society teaches personal and family preparedness as "provident living." This implies the husbanding of our resources, the wise planning of financial matters, full provision for personal health, and adequate preparation for education and career development, giving appropriate attention to home production and storage as well as the development of emotional resiliency.

. . . I hope that we understand that, while having a garden, for instance, is often useful in reducing food costs and making available delicious fresh fruits and vegetables, it does much more than this. Who can gauge the value of that special chat between daughter and Dad as they weed or water the garden? How do we evaluate the good that comes from the obvious lessons of planting, cultivating, and the eternal law of the harvest? And how do we measure the family togetherness and cooperating that must accompany successful canning? Yes, we are laying up resources in store, but perhaps the greater good is contained in the lessons of life we learn as we *live providently* and extend to our children their pioneer heritage.

. . . In like manner we could refer to all the components of personal and family preparedness, not in relation to holocaust or disaster, but in cultivating a lifestyle that is on a day-to-day basis its own reward.

Let's do these things because they are right, because they are satisfying, and because we are obedient to the counsels of the Lord. In this spirit we will be prepared for most eventualities, and the Lord will prosper and

comfort us. It is true that difficult times will come—for the Lord has foretold them—and, yes, stakes of Zion are "for a defense, and for a refuge from the storm." (D&C 115:6.) But if we live wisely and providently, we will be as safe as in the palm of His hand.

I hope that in our priesthood quorums and Relief Society meetings the concepts of personal and family preparedness are being properly taught and with the kind of positive approach that we all respond to.

*   *   *   *   *   *

Spencer W. Kimball
October Conference, 1977

. . . *Gardens can provide savings and pleasure.* We are highly pleased with the response to the planting of gardens. It is health-building, both from the raising of crops and the eating of them. It is delightful to see so many gardens all over the land, and reports come in from numerous families and individuals who have obtained much saving and pleasure in the planting of gardens. We hope this will be a permanent experience of our people, that they will raise much of what they use on their table.

*   *   *   *   *   *

Spencer W. Kimball
April Conference, 1978

With the arrival of spring we hope all of you will put in your gardens and prepare to enjoy their produce this summer. We hope you are making this a family affair, with everyone, even the little ones, assigned to something. There is so much to learn and harvest from your garden, far more than just a crop itself. We also hope that you are maintaining your year's supply of food, clothing, and where possible, some fuel and cash savings.

. . . Would you see to it that in your quorum and Relief Society meetings the principles and practices of personal and family preparedness are taught.

. . . *Gardening brings us close to nature.* Even if the tomato you eat is a two-dollar tomato, it will bring satisfaction anyway and remind us all of the law of the harvest, which is relentless in life. We do reap what we sow. Even if the plot of soil you cultivate, plant, and harvest is a small one, it brings human nature closer to nature as was the case in the beginning with our first parents.

. . .*Free agency requires self-reliance.* No amount of philosophizing, excuses, or rationalizing will ever change the fundamental need for self-reliance. . . . With this agency we can rise to glory or fall to condemnation. . . . The principle of self-reliance stands behind the Church's emphasis on personal and family preparedness.

*   *   *   *   *   *

Spencer W. Kimball
April Conference, 1978

. . . *Plant gardens.* Many have done much to beautify their homes and their yards. Many others have followed the counsel to have their own gardens wherever it is possible so that we do not lose contact with the soil and so that we can have the security of being able to provide at least some of our food and necessities.

Grow all the food that you possibly can on your own property, if water is available; berry bushes, grapevines, and fruit trees are most desirable. Plant them if your climate is right for their growth. Grow vegetables and eat those grown in your own yard. Even those residing in apartments or condominiums can generally grow a little food in pots and planters.

* * * * * *

Spencer W. Kimball
April Conference, 1979

My father practiced what he preached. He didn't just tell others to be self-reliant; we were taught to exemplify it as a family. We raised almost all of our own food. He always wanted a garden—he wanted a garden to eat from and a garden to smell. I used to pump the water by hand to water the garden, and also I learned to milk the cows, prune the fruit trees, mend the fences, and all the rest. I had two older brothers, who, I was convinced, took all the easy jobs and left me all the hard ones. But I don't complain; it made me strong.

. . . Most of us learn best what we apply in our own lives. I hope I would not be found wanting in applying basic gospel principles in my life, in my own home, with my own family. I would live the precepts of personal and family preparedness. That means having a garden, wisely managing family resources, and expanding my educational horizons. It means staying fit, replenishing the family year's supply, fixing up our property, and all the rest we have been asked of the Lord to do.

. . . "It is in the doing that the real blessing comes. Do it! That's our motto."

* * * * * *

Spencer W. Kimball
April Conference, 1981

Where you have a plot of land, however small, plant a garden. Staying close to the soil is good for the soul. Purchase your essentials wisely and carefully. Strive to save a portion of that which you earn. Do not mistake many wants for basic needs.

* * * * * *

Spencer W. Kimball
The Teachings of Spencer W. Kimball
Bookcraft, p. 372

I am not howling calamity, but I fear that a great majority of our young people, never having known calamity, depression, hunger, homelessness, joblessness, cannot conceive of such situations ever coming again. There are thousands of young families in this city who could not stand without suffering a three-months period without the threat of their home being foreclosed, their car repossessed, their electric and home equipment being taken back and themselves being reduced to unbelievable rations in the necessities.

The great difficulty is that when difficult times come, those who in normal times could lend assistance are also under the wheel of the grinding mill. It may be impossible to anticipate and prepare for the eventualities of depression, war, invasion, bombing, but we can go a long way. What I have seen with my own eyes makes me afraid not to do what I can to protect against the calamities. I went through two bank failures, two wars, major ones, loss of a job when jobs were scarce, but there has never been a time since our marriage that we did not have a few bonds or a savings account or some liquid assets on which to lean.

You have what you think adequate insurance, but are you prepared for and protected against death, illness, a long-continuing crippling illness of the breadwinner? How long can you go if the income stops? What are your reserves? How long could you make your many payments on home, car, implements, appliances? How long could you carry armloads of groceries from a cash store?

The first reaction is: We just cannot do it. We can hardly get by using every cent of income monthly. The answer is eloquent. If you can hardly get by when you are earning increasingly, well employed, well, productive, young, then how can you meet emergencies with employment curtailed, illness and other unlooked-for problems arising?

* * * * * *

Harold B. Lee
Improvement Era, May 1946

The Lord has given us in this day the greatest organization upon the face of the earth, with His power and His authority to direct it. He has given us sound principles; he has shown us the [welfare] plan and the way by which want and distress may be done away among us. He has shown us the way to brotherly love. If the afflictions which have been predicted do come upon us, they will come upon us because we have not kept the faith and because we have been disobedient and have thrown away the opportunities that our Heavenly Father has given us to prepare for the day of calamity which He foretold, over one hundred years ago, would come in this generation.

* * * * * *

Harold B. Lee
Address Delivered at Brigham Young University
Leadership Week, June 16, 1953

The only safety and security there is in this Church is in listening to the words that come from the prophets of the Lord, as if from the mouth of the Lord himself. And they have spoken; they have told us to prepare, and it is not for us to argue whether we should or whether we should not. We have the prophets today telling us what our responsibility is here and now. God help us not to turn deaf ears, but go out while the harvest is yet possible and build on a foundation such that when the rains descend, and the floods come, and the winds blow, and beat on the house, our house will have stone walls.

* * * * * *

Harold B. Lee
Welfare Meeting, October Conference, 1966

Brother Taylor has talked about storage. I think there is nothing that has been so expanded all out of the original intent as has this storage program, which is intended to teach a principle. Now one or two things we must say to you, and in some places it is getting way out of hand. Wards and stakes are not to enter into a buying and selling program to their members, and certainly it is not to be done by the Relief Society, the priesthood quorums nor any other Church units. To go to wholesalers and solicit a little better price on a can of beans or pork and beans, merely to help to save a few cents, usually for those who are able to buy themselves, and then to have somebody complain, "Well, I don't like that brand of corn," or, "I don't like that brand of peas," is not a part of the Welfare Program.

We can get into more trouble with our local grocery-men, with our taxing authorities, and with the public generally by entering into a buying and selling program of this sort, which is but competing with the corner groceryman who is struggling to keep a little life in his business. Now I think there can be more harm done than the small good that will be accomplished. We teach the principle of putting aside for the "rainy" day.

We have never laid down an exact formula for what anybody should store, and let me just make this comment: Perhaps if we think not in terms of a year's supply of what we ordinarily would use, and think more in terms of what it would take to keep us alive in case we didn't have anything else to eat, that last would be very easy to put in storage for a year. . . just enough to keep us alive if we didn't have anything else to eat. We wouldn't get fat on it, but we would live, and if you think in terms of that kind of annual storage rather than a whole year's supply of everything that you are accustomed to eat which, in most cases, is utterly impossible for the average family, I think we will come nearer to what President Clark advised us way back in 1937.

* * * * * *

Harold B. Lee
Priesthood Welfare Representatives' Seminar
November 29, 1966, Salt Lake City

I've been wondering lately if we're not placing too much emphasis on home storage and neglecting some of the things, which from my standpoint, are weightier than merely talking about food storage.

Food storage was something that was given as counsel from the Presidency of the Church. And it's come now in many places to mean merely a scheme of trying, as I told you in the last conference, of trying to save a few cents a can, for somebody that doesn't need to have that saving. In other words, he's not entitled to it, and somebody is beating his brains out trying to find out some source—wholesale or otherwise—where he can save those few cents. I have a feeling that maybe we're spending too much time on food storage. If we leave it just where the prophets left it, with a statement as to the counsel, this is it.

A woman called me the other day. I didn't want to engage in a long dissertation about her work as the supervisor of home storage. She was one of those who was organizing to contact people on food storage, to get the best price, and would sell and solicit. I said, "That's all outside, and is not a part of the welfare program.

"Now we've counseled against any Church unit engaging in the business of buying and selling. That applies not only to groceries, it applies to everything else. And that's just as fundamental and primal in the welfare program. You who've been with us from the beginning know that that's true—we've been publicizing it." She said she had never heard about it. I said, "Well, your stake president must have known about it. Your bishoprics must have known about it. If they'd come up through the ranks—if they'd been listening at all—they know we've counseled against any such procedure. We do not tolerate it. And sooner or later, if it becomes successful, that means it's big enough to be a money-making thing, then we're going to have the state looking down our neck. If it's just a piddling thing, where it isn't worth anything, why they're not going to bother us. But if it's big enough in volume to really begin to be something, where we buy in carload lots, for example, then somebody's going to pay attention on the tax side of it—and we're in trouble. It just is wrong in principle."

. . . I think I've never had so many eyebrows lifted—this speech (last conference) must have been good, because of the places where I've stepped on somebody's toes, including members of this committee. I discovered some of you were out in left field too, on food storage. That's why I speak to you as plainly as I do. Don't get outside of that circle of limitations. It's a program. Let's run our own house and keep it clean, and then let the world take care of itself.

* * * * * *

Harold B. Lee
Welfare Agricultural Meeting
April Conference, 1969

We have had those who have tried to take advantage of this home storage program by capitalizing from a commercial standpoint. We have cautioned you to avoid that, but to pursue the course nevertheless, to see that food is in your homes; and counsel your neighbors and friends to do likewise, because someone had a vision to know that this was going to be necessary, and it will be necessary in the future, and has been the savior of our people in the past.

. . . Now let's not be foolish and suppose that because the sun is shining today that there won't be clouds tomorrow. The Lord has told us by revelation some of the things that are ahead of us, and we living in the day when the fulfillment of those prophecies is now at hand, and we are startled, and yet there is nothing happening today that the prophets didn't foresee. Sometimes centuries ago, as one prophet of the Book of Mormon said: "I see in that day as though they were now present." That's revelation.

God help us to keep our own houses in order and to keep our eyes fixed upon those who preside in this Church and to follow their direction, and we won't be led astray.

President McKay attended the first regional meeting down here when I was sent with Brother Ballard to go all over the Church to introduce the program. Some of you are old enough to remember that. Brother McKay and Brother Clark said to me, and Brother Ballard: "Now you had better not start here in Salt Lake first, because these will be the hardest to convert because they are too close to us here. You start out around the out-fringes where they are a little more obedient to counsel than some of the local people." And they said: "Now your first talks will probably be your best, but your last talks will be the wisest, and you reserve your wisest talks for these folks in Salt Lake."

* * * * * *

Harold B. Lee
Welfare Agricultural Meeting
April Conference, 1970

For 30 years the leaders of this Church have been telling us to store food and to prepare for a rainy day.

We have listened, many have paid no attention, and now suddenly disaster begins to strike and some of those who have been slothful are running to the banks and taking out their savings, and buying hundreds and thousands of dollars worth of foodstuffs. The Lord has given us time to prepare, and many have.

* * * * * *

Harold B. Lee
Ensign, December 1971

A few days ago we had a faith-promoting report from a young mission president and his wife who have just been released from presiding over a mission in Peru, where recently there was experienced one of the worst calamities in the history of the world, in which an estimated seventy thousand persons were buried when an earthquake moved an entire mountain over two cities, which was completely destroyed. We had four missionaries laboring there, two in each city. When the earthquake came, they were at the Lord's business; two of our elders were teaching a gospel lesson on the outskirts of the town and the other two were in a preparation meeting in another city.

After the three terrifying days of semidarkness from the choking dust, they philosophized that this might be like the time when the Savior was crucified, when there were three days of darkness, and when he would come again, when two should be grinding at the mill, and one would be taken and the other left; two would be working in the field, and one would be taken and the other one left. (See Matt. 24:40-41.)

When an earthquake strikes, every person would be taken as he is then living—if at a movie, or a tavern, or in a drunken stupor, or whatever. But the true servants of God, who would be doing their duty, would be protected and preserved, if they would do as the Lord has counseled: to "stand ye in holy places, and be not moved," when these days should come. (D&C 87:8.)

* * * * * *

Neal A. Maxwell
New Era, January 1971

Our task is to react and to notice without over-reacting, to let life go forward without slipping into the heedlessness of those in the days of Noah. It has been asked, and well it might be, how many of us would have jeered, or at least been privately amused, by the sight of Noah building his ark.

Presumably, the laughter and the heedlessness continued until it began to rain—and kept raining. How wet some people must have been before Noah's ark suddenly seemed the only sane act in an insane, bewildering situation! To ponder signs without becoming paranoid, to be aware without frantically matching current events with expectations and using energy that should be spent in other ways—these are our tasks.

* * * * * *

Bruce R. McConkie
April Conference, 1979

I stand before the Church this day and raise the warning voice. It is a prophetic voice, for I shall say only what the apostles and prophets have spoken concerning our day.

. . . It is a voice calling upon the Lord's people to prepare for the troubles and desolations which are about to be poured out upon the world without measure.

For the moment we live in a day of peace and prosperity but it shall not ever be thus. Great trials lie ahead. All of the sorrows and perils of the past are but a foretaste of what is yet to be. And we must prepare ourselves temporally and spiritually.

. . . There will be earthquakes and floods and famines. The waves of the sea shall heave themselves beyond their bounds, the clouds shall withhold their rain, and the crops of the earth shall wither and die.

. . . It is one of the sad heresies of our time that peace will be gained by weary diplomats as they prepare treaties of compromise, or that the Millennium will be ushered in because men will learn to live in peace and to keep the commandments, or that the predicted plagues and promised desolations of latter days can in some way be avoided.

We must do all we can to proclaim peace, to avoid war, to heal disease, to prepare for natural disasters— but with it all, that which is to be shall be.

. . . We must maintain our own health, sow our own gardens, store our own food, educate and train ourselves to handle the daily affairs of life. No one else can work out our salvation for us, either temporally or spiritually.

. . . We do not say that all of the Saints will be spared and saved from the coming day of desolation. But we do say there is no promise of safety and no promise of security except for those who love the Lord and who are seeking to do all that he commands.

It may be, for instance, that nothing except the power of faith and the authority of the priesthood can save individuals and congregations from the atomic holocausts that surely shall be.

And so we raise the warning voice and say: Take heed; prepare; watch and be ready. There is no security in any course except the course of obedience and conformity and righteousness.

. . . Knowing what we know, and having the light and understanding that has come to us, we must—as individuals and as a Church—use our talents, strengths, energies, abilities, and means to prepare for whatever may befall us and our children.

. . . We do not know when the calamities and troubles of the last days will fall upon any of us as individuals or upon bodies of the Saints. The Lord deliberately withholds from us the day and hour of his coming and of the tribulations which shall precede it—all as part of the testing and probationary experiences of mortality. He simply tells us to watch and be ready.

We can rest assured that if we have done all in our power to prepare for whatever lies ahead, he will then help us with whatever else we need.

* * * * * *

Bruce R. McConkie
April Conference, 1980

Nor are the days of our greatest sorrows and our deepest sufferings all behind us. They too lie ahead. We shall yet face greater perils, we shall yet be tested with more severe trials, and we shall yet weep more tears of sorrow than we have ever known before.

. . . But the vision of the future is not all sweetness and light and peace. All that is yet to be shall go forward in the midst of greater evils and perils and desolations than have been known on earth at any time.

* * * * * *

Thomas S. Monson
Ensign, September 1986

Faithful compliance with these revealed welfare principles and practices have preserved lives in times of crises. An example is found in the response of Church members to the 1985 earthquake that devastated parts of Mexico City. Church members and leaders rose to the occasion, drawing on their own preparedness efforts to help themselves and others around them.

Another example occurred at the time of the Idaho Teton Dam disaster in the summer of 1976, when thousands of Latter-day Saints gave of their own reserves to those whose every belonging was swept away in the floodwaters. We remember also the massive effort of Church members following World War II when our own prophet-leader, President Benson, then a member of the Council of the Twelve, administered the distribution of more than seventy-five train-carloads of commodities to needy members in war-ravaged Europe. These outpourings of humanitarian service were made possible by the faithful adherence of Church members to the very principles we have just reviewed.

. . . President Spencer W. Kimball further taught concerning self-reliance: "The responsibility for each person's social, emotional, spiritual, physical, or economic well-being rests first upon himself, second upon his family, and third upon the Church if he is a faithful member thereof.

. . . Perhaps no counsel has been repeated more often than how to *manage wisely our income.* Consumer debt in some nations of the world is at staggering levels. Too many in the Church have failed to avoid unnecessary debt. They have little, if any, financial reserve. The solution is to budget, to live within our means, and to save some for the future.

. . . Recent surveys of Church members have shown a serious erosion in the number of families who have *a year's supply* of life's necessities. Most members plan to do it. Too few have begun. We must sense again the spirit of the persistent instruction given by Elder Harold B. Lee as he spoke to the members in 1943: "Again there came counsel in 1942. . . . 'We renew our counsel, said the leaders of the Church, and repeat our instruction: Let every Latter-day Saint that has land, produce some valuable essential foodstuff thereon and then preserve it.' . . . Let me ask you leaders who are here today: In 1937 did you store in your own basements and in your own private storehouses and granaries sufficient for a year's supply? You city dwellers, did you in 1942 heed what was said from this stand?" (In Conference Report, April 1943, p. 127.)

. . . Undergirding this pointed call is the stirring appeal from our own living prophet, President Ezra Taft Benson, wherein he has given specific suggestions for putting these teachings into action:

"From the standpoint of food production, storage, handling, and the Lord's counsel, wheat should have high priority. . . . Water, of course, is essential. Other basics could include honey or sugar, legumes, milk products or substitutes, and salt or its equivalent. The revelation to produce and store food may be as essential to our temporal welfare today as boarding the ark was to the people in the days of Noah." (*Ensign,* Nov. 1980, p. 33.)

As has been said so often, the best storehouse system that the Church could devise would be for every family to store a year's supply of needed food, clothing, and, where possible, the other necessities of life.

In the early church, Paul wrote to Timothy, "If any provide not for his own, and specially for those of his own house, he hath denied the faith, and is worse than an infidel." (1 Tim. 5:8.) It is our sacred duty to *care for our families, including our extended families.*

* * * * * *

Henry D. Moyle

We are constantly charged with preparation in time of plenty against want in time of need.

* * * * * *

Russel M. Nelson
April Conference, 1986

An important part of the Lord's storehouse is maintained as a year's supply, stored, where possible, in the homes of faithful families of the Church.

* * * * * *

Glenn L. Pace
Quoting Marion G. Romney
April Conference, 1986

He made the process sound so simple. "Brother Pace, don't make things so complicated! All we have been trying to do is make our people self-reliant, because the more self-reliant one is, the more able to serve he becomes, and the more he serves, the greater his sanctification."

* * * * * *

Boyd K. Packer
Scandinavian Area Conference
Copenhagen, Denmark, August 1976

I would like to mention in more detail the flood in Idaho. President Kimball has mentioned our visit there. When that earthwork dam collapsed, there were seventeen miles of water backed up behind it. All of that water was released on the valleys below. It was a quiet Saturday morning, a beautiful sunny day. There were 7,800 people living in the immediate path of the flood, and another 25,000 or 30,000 further down the valley. Almost all of them are Latter-day Saints.

. . . Wilford Ward, which was at the mouth of the canyon, was washed away—all of it—all of the houses, all of the barns, all of the gardens, everything—a whole ward gone. The chapel was gone. A mile or two downstream, Sugar City was washed away. The stake center and a few houses stood, but they were subject to terrible destruction. In all, 790 homes were completely destroyed. Most of them disappeared without a trace, except for the cement foundations. Eight hundred other others were severely damaged, along with churches and schools and houses of business.

. . . President Kimball has mentioned what happened to the people. Only six died by drowning—six of about 35,000. How could there be such a terrible destruction with such little loss of life? They couldn't go up on the roof and be saved, because the houses were washed away. Most of them had several miles to go to high ground. Now, why did they live? Because they were warned! They didn't have very long, but they were warned; and every man that was warned warned his neighbor.

. . . But it was a miracle of tremendous proportion because as Latter-day Saints, we learn to heed the warnings. When there is a terrible destruction, we will warn our neighbors. There is page after page of miracles. Of how a father heard of the warning, but his children were scattered over the farm. He was in town, and his wife had no car. But they were saved. Miracles of how the aged and the infirm and the children were rescued. One expert said that there should have been about 5,300 people killed. But there were six, because they were warned and they heeded the warning.

* * * * * *

Boyd K. Packer
Amsterdam Area Conference, August 1976

It was a beautiful, calm Saturday morning, all the farmers were getting their crops in and working on their farms. There came a break in the dam, up in the mountains, seventeen miles of water backed up behind it. And finally it collapsed. The first community at the mouth of the canyon was Wilford. There were 7,800 people living just below the mountains, and down the valley a ways 25,000 or 30,000 more, almost all of them Latter-day Saints. Wilford Ward was washed away—all of it, and all of the houses. The chapel stood, with just the walls and the sagging roof. But there was not a home, or a barn, or a garden, or anything left of Wilford Ward.

A mile or two downstream, Sugar City was washed away. The stake center and a few houses stood, but they were terribly damaged. In all, 790 homes disappeared, most of them without a trace. Some cement foundations were all you could find. Eight hundred other homes were badly damaged, as were schools and churches. Fourteen of our chapels were damaged or destroyed. But then you know about floods here, from your history, and sometimes you may be anxious about them.

. . . Now what about the people? As President Kimball told you, there were six lives lost by drowning. The experts say there should have been 5,300 deaths. But there were six: one a fisherman just below the dam; two heard the warning but wouldn't leave until it was too late; three went back to get something.

What about the other thousands? They were all saved. Why? Because they heeded the warning. They had almost no time when the warning first went out, but Latter-day Saints are trained to heed the warnings. We are a people who are trained to be obedient. We sustain our leaders. We uphold them and we obey them and we heed the warnings.

. . . You know, it is a great experience to listen to the miracles that took place in Idaho. One fourteen-year-old boy was in Rexburg when he heard the warning. He knew his little sister was home on the farm, sick in bed. When it was all over with, they were both up at the college safe.

One of the teachers at the college was in his office that morning, and someone tapped at the door and said, "Turn on your radio. There is something happening." He thought of his wife out on the farm and his boys out

irrigating, and he had the only car. There was no possible time for him to get there. How were they saved? They were warned by their neighbors. They were rescued by their neighbors. He prayed them out of the flood. Did you know you could do that?

* * * * * *

Boyd K. Packer
April Conference, 1982

Let me give you a modern-day example. President Kimball has been President of the Church for eight years. In virtually every conference sermon he has included at least a sentence telling us to clean up, paint up, and fix up our property. Many of us have paid little attention to the counsel.

Question: Why would a prophet tell us to do that? Has he no great prophecies to utter?

But, is that not a form of prophecy? For has he not said to us over and over again, "Take good care of your material possessions, for the day will come when they will be difficult, if not impossible, to replace."

. . . For some reason, we expect to hear, particularly in welfare sessions, some ominous great predictions of calamities to come. Instead, we hear quiet counsel on ordinary things which, if followed, will protect us in times of great calamity.

* * * * * *

L. Tom Perry
October Conference, 1980

Having a one-year supply must be moved up on the family priority list. How it is obtained must be considered again. Can more of it be the result of our own labors in making our own clothes, increasing our garden yield, and preserving our own food?

* * * * * *

L. Tom Perry
April Conference, 1981

It is time to teach the basics—again. It is time to make the number one priority of our welfare efforts personal and family preparedness. We must prepare now so that in time of need more of our members will be able to draw upon their own preparedness and not have to seek assistance from the Church.

. . . Personal and family preparedness planning must begin with the family executive committee. Planning must be tailored to fit the circumstances of each family. Consideration must be given to their unique requirements in career development, financial and resource management, education, physical health, home production and storage, and social, emotional, and spiritual strength.

. . . How grateful I am for a father who had the patience to teach me the art of gardening. How frustrating it must have been in this teaching process to find a neat row of weeds still in the ground and a pile of dead carrots on the ground after I'd completed one of my assignments. Our family was taught not only the art of stacking and rotating cans and bottles on shelves, but also how to grow and replace the fruits and vegetables necessary to fill the empty cans and bottles again.

. . . With such alarming results we must remind ourselves that the Church welfare system was never designed or intended to care for the healthy member who, as a result of his poor management or lack of preparation, has found himself in difficulty. It was designed to assist the membership in case of a large, physical disaster, such as an earthquake or a flood. It was designed to assist the ill, the injured, the incapacitated, and to rehabilitate them to a productive life. In far too many cases, members who should be making use of their own preparedness provisions are finding that there is nothing there and that they have to turn to the Church.

*   *   *   *   *   *

H. Burke Peterson
October Conference, 1975

To foster the economic self-sufficiency of the Latter-day Saint families, fathers and mothers, priesthood and Relief Society leaders are encouraged first to focus upon family preparedness, an important part of which is home production—canning, gardening, sewing, making household items—and also upon home storage, on the need for Saints to have a year's supply of food, clothing, and, where possible, fuel. All this is accomplished as fathers, mothers, and children respond to priesthood direction and prepare for the eventualities that lie ahead. Fathers receive instruction through their priesthood quorums, mothers from their husbands and through Relief Society's program for provident living.

. . . Therefore, family preparedness, with home production and storage, must be the way the majority of our families take care of themselves.

. . . The study revealed that only about 5 percent of our Church members had a year's supply of meat products. Only 3 percent had a year's supply of dried or canned fruits or vegetables. Approximately 18 percent had a year's supply of grains. In the milk group, only three families in a hundred had a year's supply of canned or powdered milk. On the average, about 30 percent of the Church had a two-months supply of food; the remainder had little or none.

These survey statistics indicate that most Church members are not prepared to meet month-to-month problems and future economic trials. Clearly, in this area of home production and storage, it is extremely important that priesthood and Relief Society leaders

and all Latter-day Saints place greater emphasis on home storage—on obtaining and carefully storing a year's supply of food, clothing, and, where possible, fuel. In the area of home production, we would hope that members would heed the admonition of the prophets and, where possible, grow a garden, sew their own clothing, make household items, and, in general, become as self-sufficient as possible to prepare against the days to come. In the words of President Kimball, "We are pleased that many people are planting gardens and fruit trees and are buying canning jars and lids. . . . We congratulate those families who are listening and doing.

"We make a conscientious effort to look out for our own members, and we teach them to practice economy, to store a year's supply of basic commodities." (*Ensign*, May 1975, pp. 5-6.)

*   *   *   *   *   *

H. Burke Peterson
October Conference, 1978

In the area of home production and storage, we still have the year's supply room in the basement with the sign designating it as the "Peterson Family Store." However, our garden and year's supply program is not the same as it was fifteen years ago. Our family store reflects the needs of two adults, one child, and many visitors instead of the needs of two adults and five children, as it did in years past.

*   *   *   *   *   *

Mark E. Peterson
April Conference, 1981

There are many very good people who keep most of the Lord's commandments with respect to the virtuous side of life, but who overlook His commandments in temporal things. They do not heed His warning to prepare for a possible future emergency, apparently feeling that in the midst of all this trouble "it won't happen to us." It is not always the other fellow's problem. It is our problem also whenever there is economic trouble afloat.

To prepare for the future is part of God's eternal plan, both spiritually and temporally. To protect ourselves against reversals and hardships is only good sense.

. . . That great program teaches us to put away one year's supply of our necessities—not the frills and the superfluities. We can get along without the frosting on the cake, can't we, or the whipped cream on the apple pie?

And if necessary we can get along just fine without either the cake or the pie, can't we, and just be glad for the staples of life?

. . . But the most important storehouses in the entire welfare plan are those that are within the walls of our own homes. We must provide our own storehouses for our own families in our own homes as far as possible to meet any rainy days that may come our way.

. . . He teaches us to be self-reliant and industrious, to plan ahead, to provide for possible hard times, to avoid obligations unless we are sure we can handle them, and then *to serve him* with such devotion that He will be pleased to augment all of our own earnest efforts.

* * * * * *

Marion G. Romney
April Conference, 1976
Quoting Brigham Young

". . . If we are to be saved in an ark, as Noah and his family were, it will be because we build it. . . .

"My faith does not lead me," President Young continued, "to think the Lord will provide us with roast pigs, bread already buttered, etc., he will give us the ability to raise the grain, to obtain the fruits of the earth, to make habitations, to procure a few boards to make a box, and when harvest comes, giving us the grain, it is for us to preserve it—to save the wheat until we have one, two, five, or seven years' provisions on hand, until there is enough of the staff of life saved by the people to bread themselves and those who will come here seeking for safety. . . . [The fulfillment of that prophecy is yet in the future.]

"Ye Latter-day Saints, learn to sustain yourselves. . . .

"Implied faith and confidence in God is for you and me to do everything we can to sustain and preserve ourselves. . . .

"You have learned a good deal, it is true; but learn more; learn to sustain yourselves, lay up grain and flour, and save it against a day of scarcity. . . .

"Instead of searching after what the Lord is going to do for us, let us inquire what we can do for ourselves." (*Discourses of Brigham Young,* Deseret Book, 1966 ed., pp. 291-93.)

* * * * * *

Marion G. Romney
April Conference, 1979

Now I would like to repeat what you have heard a thousand times, more or less, about taking care of yourselves. You ought to know now, more than at any previous time, to make sure that you are prepared to go through a period of stress on the resources you have provided for yourselves. The necessity to do this may come any day. I hope it will not come too soon. In fact, I hope it doesn't come in my lifetime. But it will come sooner or later.

Never forget this matter of providing for yourselves,

even though you don't hear as much about it now as you did a few years ago. Remember that it is still a fundamental principle, one that has been taught the Saints ever since they came to these valleys of the mountains. We have always been urged to provide ourselves, in the day of harvest, enough to last until the next harvest. Be sure that you do so now. Be prepared to take care of yourselves through a period of need.

I don't know how things will work out. People say to me, "What will we do? If we have a year's supply and others do not, it will be gone in a day." Well, it will last as long as it lasts, but I'm not worried about that. If we will do what the Lord tells us to do, he will take care of us all right.

* * * * * *

Marion G. Romney
Ensign, September 1979

Communism is Satan's counterfeit for the Gospel plan, and . . . it is an avowed enemy of the God of this land. Communism is the greatest anti-Christ power in the world today and therefore the greatest menace not only to our peace but to our preservation as a free people.

* * * * * *

Marion G. Romney
Ensign, April 1981

It has also been my intention to encourage all Latter-day Saints to review again their personal and family preparedness and to implement immediately the principles and practices that will ensure their self-sufficiency. If we will discuss these truths in our family councils and make a plan to do all in our power to live these principles, we shall all enjoy the promise of the Lord, "If ye are prepared ye shall not fear." (D&C 38:30.)

. . . What, then, does it mean to be prepared? Someone proposed a serious question to me a few years ago by asking, "What is the most important item to have stored in your year's supply?" My response was seriously given—"personal righteousness."

. . . It is important for us to have, as we have been counseled, a year's supply of food and clothing, and where possible, fuel. We have also been counseled that we should have a reserve of cash to meet emergencies and to carry adequate health, home, and life insurance. Personal and family preparedness, however, is much broader than these tangibles. It must include proper attitudes, a willingness to forego luxuries, prayerful consideration of all major purchases, and learning to live within our means.

Sadly, surveys show that there are many of us who have not followed this counsel, believing evidently, that the Church can and will take care of us.

* * * * * *

Marion G. Romney
October Conference, 1982

Can we see how critical self-reliance becomes when looked upon as the prerequisite to service, when we also know service is what Godhood is all about? Without self-reliance one cannot exercise these innane desires to serve. How can we give if there is nothing there? Food for the hungry cannot come from empty shelves. Money to assist the needy cannot come from an empty purse. Support and understanding cannot come from the emotionally starved. Teaching cannot come from the unlearned. And most important of all, spiritual guidance cannot come from the spiritually weak.

* * * * * *

Barbara B. Smith
April Conference, 1976

Relief Society officers are in a position to materially assist the women of the Church to respond obediently to the advice of our leaders regarding home production and storage, that each family may be prepared to take care of its basic needs for a minimum of one year. Latter-day Saint women should be busily engaged in growing, producing, and conserving food, within their capabilities to do so. Relief Society should help them be provident in the use of the resources available to them, however great or small these resources may be. By *provident,* I mean wise, frugal, prudent, making provision for the future while attending to immediate needs.

. . . Each ward or branch Relief Society presidency should make an assessment of the general circumstances of the sisters living within their area and prepare a one-year plan for homemaking meeting instruction to be given on subjects relating to home production and storage, according to the needs and conditions of the women. These classes could include the following guidelines to provident living:

1. How to save systematically for emergencies and home storage.
2. How to, what to, and where to store.
3. How to store seeds, prepare soil, acquire proper tools for gardening.
4. How to grow your own vegetables.
5. How to can and dry foods.
6. How to teach and help your family eat foods needed for physical health.
7. How to do basic machine and hand sewing, mending, and clothing remodeling.
8. How to plan and prepare nutritious, appetizing meals using the resources available, and foods from home storage shelves.

The resources of libraries, extension services, and government agencies should be wisely used. Instruction should be given that will help each sister understand how to make a good home storage plan in council with her husband, that he might direct their family.

. . . The principles of family preparedness and a woman's part in them were not given for our time alone. I consider the woman described in the thirty-first chapter of Proverbs a provident woman. Recall her wisdom, prudence, frugality, and preparation, as "She seeketh wool, and flax, and worketh willingly with her hands. . . .

"With the fruit of her hands she planteth a vineyard. . . .

"She layeth her hands to the spindle, and her hands hold the distaff. . . .

"She is not afraid of the snow for her household: for all her household are clothed with scarlet. . . .

"She looketh well to the ways of her household, and eateth not the bread of idleness." (See Prov. 31:13-31.)

* * * * * *

Barbara B. Smith
October Conference, 1976

My dear brothers and sisters, last July six stake Relief Society presidents visited me in my office; they were all from Idaho stakes affected by the Teton flood.

They spoke of the labor and love given by thousands of priesthood volunteers and also of the service of countless Relief Society women who washed, scrubbed, cleaned, prepared food, cared for children, and performed other essential services for victims of that terrible disaster.

As those sisters spoke, several images came to my mind. I was reminded of one of the beautiful sculptures of the Relief Society's Nauvoo monument—a woman with hands outstretched in an attitude of compassion, typifying the woman described in Proverbs:

"She stretcheth out her hand to the poor: yea, she reacheth forth her hands to the needy." (Prov. 31:20.)

. . . I recalled my own visit to the flood area, where I saw a cultural hall with tables with good clothing, clearly sized and marked; another room with neatly stacked food—cans of wheat, dehydrated milk, bottled fruit, nonfood items—all donated by individuals acting in spontaneous compassion and generosity. I remembered the spirit of love and unity, as members in nearby areas not affected by the flood opened their homes and shared their food and other supplies with flood victims.

I thought at the time what a blessing it was that those who had been obedient to the counsel of the Brethren had sufficient personal supplies to share with the flood victims. Through this hard experience, lessons in preparedness and provident living were learned for the entire Church.

. . .1. *Basic Food Storage.* Included in the year's supply of basic foods should be life-sustaining foods that store well for a long time: grains (wheat, rice, corn, or other of the cereal grains); dried milk, dried fish or protein vegetables such as beans and peas and other fresh, canned, dried, or pickled fruit or vegetables; sugar or a sugar substitute such as honey; some form of fats; salt; and water. Fresh taro or sweet potato, and live pigs, chickens, or fish might be considered as a supply in some area of the world where it is difficult to store food. Remember that regular use of whole grains is important in building a digestive tolerance for roughage.

2. *Basic Clothing and Fuel Storage.*

3. *Emergency Storage.* You may wish to consider storing, where they could be picked up at a moment's notice, such items as water, food needing no refrigeration or cooking, medications needed by family members, a change of clothing for each family member, a first-aid booklet and first-aid supplies, an ax, shovel, and blanket. These would be used when a family or individual has only a short time to flee a disaster or needs to stay in a sheltered area within the home. It is also wisdom to have the family's important papers and documents together where they could be picked up at a moment's notice.

4. *Expanded Storage.* Families may also wish to expand their basic storage to include foods and other daily essentials that would supply total nutritional needs and allow for variety and personal preferences in diet and living. These would be things normally used every day, for which frequent shopping is done.

. . . I repeat, home storage should consist of a year's supply of basic food, clothing, and where possible, fuel. After this goal is reached, emergency and expanded storage is desirable.

In all of our storage, quality products, proper containers and storage facilities, proper storage temperature, and regular rotation are important considerations. Some of the recent disasters in which Church members have been involved show that there is a need for diversification in *places* of storage and in types of containers. Perhaps not all storage should be concentrated in one area of the house, not all should be stored in tin or plastic containers, not all in glass containers.

I outlined in the April 1976 welfare services meeting eight suggested topics for Relief Society homemaking mini-classes. I repeat these by way of review:

How to save systematically for emergencies and home storage.

How to, what to, and where to store.

How to store seeds, prepare soil, acquire proper tools for gardening.

How to grow your own vegetables.

How to can and dry foods.

How to teach and help your family eat foods needed for physical health.

How to do basic machine and hand sewing, mending, and clothing remodeling.

How to plan and prepare nutritious, appetizing meals, using the resources available and foods from home storage shelves.

May I also strongly urge stake and district Relief Society leaders to encourage miniclass instruction on how to use the basic food storage items in daily diets. I ask Relief Society leaders to secure and study approved materials on home storage appropriate to local culture, climate, and area; to counsel with local priesthood leaders and make realistic storage plans available to the people in their area. Plans for storage may vary according to the circumstances of individuals or families. But always the guidelines will be helpful that are set forth in the Church Welfare Services Department bulletin, *Essentials of Home Storage,* available through Church Distribution. Local university and government departments could also be a source of help.

*　*　*　*　*　*

Barbara B. Smith
October Conference, 1980

Note Joseph's obedience to the Lord's warning of impending famine, that "the land perish not through the famine" (Gen. 41:36). "Joseph gathered corn as the sand of the sea" (Gen. 41:49) during the seven plenteous years against the seven years of famine."

*　*　*　*　*　*

Barbara B. Smith
April Conference, 1981

I have thought about the emergency preparation necessary when Noah's ark was made ready. Noah must have achieved the most effective welfare planning in the history of mankind when he very carefully followed the Lord's counsel and built the ark. His wife and their sons undoubtedly worked and planned with him so that the blessings of the Lord might be theirs. Just think of preparing a year's supply for those multitudes of animals which were brought into the ark. Noah and his family must have been able to plan and provide in such a way that they could find pleasure in their efforts (selecting just the right two of each animal), adventure in their voyage (surely there were new little furry creatures almost weekly), and joy as the splendor of the very first rainbow filled the sky, and the Lord's promise was fulfilled.

*　*　*　*　*　*

Joseph Smith
Teachings of the Prophet Joseph Smith

The time is soon coming, when no man will have any peace but in Zion and her stakes.

I saw armies arrayed against armies. I saw blood, desolation, fires. . . . These things are at our doors. . . . I do not know how soon these things will take place; but with a view of them, shall I cry peace? No; I will lift up my voice and testify of them. How long you will have good crops, and the famine be kept off, I do not know; when the fig tree leaves, know then that the summer is nigh at hand.

* * * * * *

N. Eldon Tanner
October Conference, 1979

May I comment on two of these elements. Nothing seems so certain as the unexpected in our lives. With rising medical costs, health insurance is the only way most families can meet serious accident, illness, or maternity costs, particularly those for premature births. Life insurance provides income continuation when the provider prematurely dies. Every family should make provision for proper health and life insurance.

. . . *Constancy –2: Live on less than you earn.* I have discovered that there is no way that you can ever earn *more* than you can spend. I am convinced that it is not the amount of money an individual earns that brings peace of mind as much as it is having *control* of his money. Money can be an obedient servant but a harsh taskmaster. Those who structure their standard of living to allow a little surplus, control their circumstances. Those who spend a little more than they earn are controlled by their circumstances. They are in bondage. President Grant once said: "If there is any one thing that will bring peace and contentment into the human heart, and into the family, it is to live within our means. And if there is any one thing that is grinding and discouraging and disheartening, it is to have debts and obligations that one cannot meet" (*Gospel Standards,* Salt Lake City: *Improvement Era,* 1941, p. 111).

The key to spending less than we earn is simple — it is called discipline. Whether early in life or late, we must all eventually learn to discipline ourselves, our appetites, and our economic desires. How blessed is he who learns to spend less than he earns and puts something away for a rainy day.

* * * * * *

A. Theodore Tuttle
April Conference, 1978

Let every head of every household see to it that he has on hand enough food and clothing, and, where possible, fuel also, for at least a year ahead. . . . Let every man who has a garden spot, garden it; every man who owns a farm, farm it." (In *Conference Report,* Apr. 1937, p. 26.)

Cash is not food, it is not clothing, it is not coal, it is not shelter; and we have got to the place where no matter how much cash we have, we cannot secure those things in the quantities which we may need. . . . All that you can be certain you will have is that which you produce.

* * * * * *

Wilford Woodruff
Journal of Discourses

The day will come when if this people do not lay up their bread they will be sorry for it. (President Wilford Woodruff in *Journal of Discourses,* vol. 18, p. 127.)

So far as our temporal matters are concerned, we have got to go to work and provide for ourselves. The day will come when, as we have been told, we shall all see the necessity of making our own shoes and clothing and raising our own food, and uniting together to carry out the purposes of the Lord. . . . I therefore say to you, my brethren and sisters, prepare for that which is to come. . . . (President Wilford Woodruff, *Discourses* [Salt Lake City: Bookcraft, 1946], pp. 166-7.)

* * * * * *

Brigham Young
Journal of Discourses

If you are without bread, how much wisdom can you boast, and of what real utility are your talents, if you cannot produce for yourselves and save against a day of scarcity those substances designed to sustain your natural lives?

I have proven this many a time . . . I have plenty on hand, and shall have plenty, if I keep giving it away. More than two hundred persons eat from my provisions every day, besides my family and those who work for me. I intend to keep doing so, that my bread may hold out, for if I do not I shall come short. Do you believe that principle? I know it is true, because I have proven it so many times." (*Journal of Discourses,* vol. 3, pp. 332-33.)

Brethren, learn. You have learned a good deal, it is true; but learn more; learn to sustain yourselves; lay up grain and flour, and save it against a day of scarcity. Sisters . . . aid your husbands in storing it up against a day of want, and always have a year's or two, provision on hand. (Brigham Young, *Discourses,* 1943 ed., p. 293.)

The time will come that gold will hold no comparison in value to a bushel of wheat. (Brigham Young, in *Journal of Discourses,* vol. 1, p. 250, 1943 ed., p. 298.)

* * * * * *

Brigham Young
Journal of Discourses
Quoted by Victor L. Brown
October Conference, 1980

I fear we today are somewhat like those referred to by President Brigham Young in this quotation:

"We have seen one grasshopper war before this. Then we had two years of it. We are having two years now. Suppose we have good crops next year, the people will think less of this visitation than they do now; and still less the next year; until in four or five years it will be almost gone from their minds. We are capable of being perfectly independent of these insects. If we had thousands on thousands of bushels of wheat, rye, and barley, and corn we might have said to them, [that is, the insects] 'you may go, we are not going to plant for you.' Then we could have plowed up the ground, put in the manure, and let the land rest, and the grasshoppers would not have destroyed the fruits of our labors which could have been directed to the beautifying of Zion and making our habitations places of loveliness." (In *Journal of Discourses*, 12:242.)

. . ."I believe the Latter-day Saints are the best people on the earth of whom we have any knowledge. Still, I believe that we are, in many things, very negligent, slothful and slow to obey the words of the Lord. Many seem to act upon the faith that God will sustain us instead of our trying to sustain ourselves. We are frightened at seeing the grasshoppers coming and destroying our crops. . . . I remember saying in the School of the Prophets, that I would rather the people would exercise a little more sense and save means to provide for themselves, instead of squandering it away and asking the Lord to feed them. In my reflections I have carried this matter a considerable length. I have paid attention to the counsel that has been given me. For years past it has been sounded in my ears, year after year, to lay up grain, so that we might have an abundance in the day of want. Perhaps the Lord would bring a partial famine on us; perhaps a famine would come upon our neighbors. I have been told that He might bring just such a time as we are now having. But suppose I had taken no heed to this counsel, and had not regarded the coming time, what would have been my condition to-day.

. . ."View the actions of the Latter-day Saints on this matter, and their neglect of the counsel given; and suppose the Lord would allow these insects to destroy our crops this season and the next, what would be the result? I can see death, misery and want on the faces of this people. But some may say, 'I have faith the Lord will turn them away.' What ground have we to hope this? Have I my good reason to say to my Father in heaven, 'Fight my battles,' when He has given me the sword to wield, the arm and the brain that I can fight for myself? Can I ask Him to fight my battles and sit quietly down waiting for Him to do so? I cannot. I can pray the people to hearken to wisdom, to listen to counsel; but to ask God to do for me that which I can do for myself is preposterous to my mind. Look at the Latter-day Saints. We have had our fields laden with grain for years; and if we had been so disposed, our bins might have been filled to overflowing, and with seven years' provisions on hand we might have disregarded the ravages of these insects, and have gone to the canyon and got our lumber, procured the materials, and built up and beautified our places, instead of devoting our time to fighting and endeavoring to replace that which has been lost through their destructiveness. We might have made our fences, improved our buildings, beautified Zion, let our ground rest, and prepared for the time when these insects would have gone. But now the people are running distracted here and there. . . . They are in want and in trouble, and they are perplexed. They do not know what to do. They have been told what to do, but they did not hearken to this counsel." (In *Journal of Discourses,* 12:240-41.)

President Young goes on to say: "We must learn to listen to the whispering of the Holy Spirit, and the counsels of the servants of God, until we come to the unity of the faith. If we had obeyed counsel we would have had granaries today, and they would have been full of grain; and we would have had wheat and oats and barley for ourselves and for our animals, to last us for years." (In *Journal of Discourses,* 12:241.)

Quoting further from President Young: "When Moses was on the mount they [the Israelites] went to Aaron and inquired where Moses was, and demanded gods to go before them. And Aaron told them to bring him their ear rings and their jewelry, and they did so, and he made of them a golden calf; and the people ran around it, and said these be the gods which brought us out of the land of Egypt. How much credit was due to them? Just as much as to us, for not saving our grain when we had an abundance, and when grasshoppers come, crying, 'Lord turn them away and save us.' It is just as consistent as for a man on board a steamboat on the wide ocean to say, I will show you what faith I have, and then to jump overboard, crying, 'Lord save me.' It may not seem so daring; but is it any more inconsistent than to throw away and waste the substance the Lord has given us, and when we come to want, crying to Him for what we have wasted and squandered? The Lord has been blessing us all the time, and He asks us why we have not been blessing ourselves." (In *Journal of Discourses,* 12:243.)

* * * * * *

"The only safety and security there is in this church is in listening to the words that come from the Prophets of the Lord, as if from the mouth of the Lord himself. And they have spoken. They have told us to prepare, and it is not for us to argue whether we should or whether we should not. We have the Prophets today telling us what our responsibility is here and now. God help us not to turn deaf ears, but go out while the harvest is yet possible and build on a foundation such that when the rains descend, and the floods come, and the winds blow and beat on the house, our house will have stone walls." (Harold B. Lee, Brigham Young University, Leadership Week, June 16, 1953.)

Thousands of Utahns answered the call for help and lined State Street in Salt Lake City with nearly a million sandbags stretching over five miles to help contain the raging floodwaters. The Utah flood during the spring of 1983 is the worst natural disaster in Utah's history. (May 1983, Salt Lake City, Utah.)

Salt Lake City, generally known as "Crossroads of the West," became "Venice of the West" with streets being turned into a waterland of canals and bridges. Record runoff from major mountain streams and unseasonably heavy rain contributed to Salt Lake's flood. The flow of water down Salt Lake streets always peaked about midnight, after a daytime of hot sun in the mountains melted more of the snowpack. The "river" eventually channeled into the Great Salt Lake, some ten miles away.

State Street, Salt Lake City, Utah, May 1983.

A "Hurricane Warning" means that hurricane winds of 74 miles an hour or higher, or a combination of dangerously high water and very rough seas, are expected in a specific coastal area within 24 hours. If you hear this, begin precautionary actions immediately. Unless advised to evacuate, stay indoors during a hurricane. Travel is extremely dangerous when wind and tides are whipping through your area.
Hurricane Hilda, New Orleans, Louisiana, 1964. American Red Cross photo.

When a nuclear weapon explodes near enough to the ground for its fireball to touch the ground, it forms a crater. Many thousands of tons of earth from the crater of a large explosion are pulverized into trillions of particles. These particles are contaminated by radioactive atoms produced by the nuclear explosion.

Thousands of tons of the particles are carried up into a mushroom-shaped cloud, miles above the earth. These radioactive particles then fall out of the mushroom cloud, or out of the dispersing cloud of particles blown by the winds, thus becoming fallout.

United States Department of Defense photo.

NOTES

BOOKS BY BARRY AND LYNETTE CROCKETT

This popular series of books by *Barry and Lynette Crockett* contain the most complete, reliable, and up-to-date information available on all aspects of family emergency preparedness. Each lavishly illustrated book is filled with facts, figures, simple step-by-step lists and checklists to help you better prepare!

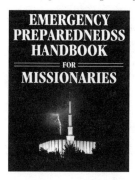

Emergency Preparedness Handbook for Missionaries ($7.95). Handy, concise, quick-reference guide clearly explains what actions to take before, during, and after various natural and manmade disasters. Compact size fits easily in missionary scripture tote bag or in dash-box of car!

Family Emergency Plan, Vol. 1 ($9.95). Contains simple outlines and worksheets for a complete family emergency response plan. All you do is fill in the blanks!

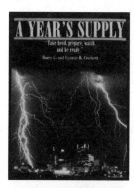

A Year's Supply ($11.95). A practical and simple guide to help you obtain and carefully store a year's supply of food, clothing, fuel and other basic necessities. A family must!

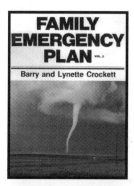

Family Emergency Plan, Vol. 2 ($9.95). Outlines what families should do before, during, and after earthquakes, tidal waves, volcanoes, landslides, avalanches, dam failures, structure fires, power failures, hazardous material accidents, and civil disturbances!

72-Hour Family Emergency Preparedness Checklist ($8.95). An invaluable guide to help you assemble a quality, inexpensive 72-hour kit for each family member.

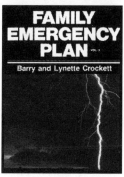

Family Emergency Plan, Vol. 3 ($9.95). Actions to take before, during, and after hurricanes, tornadoes, lightning and severe thunderstorms, floods, winter storms, drought and extreme heat, nuclear and radiological emergencies, and developing national emergencies!

Please select the books you want:

Title/Description	How Many	$Amount
Emergency Preparedness Handbook for Missionaires @$7.95 ea.		
A Year's Supply @$11.95 ea.		
72-Hour Family Emergency Preparedness Checklist @$8.95 ea.		
Family Emergency Plan, Vol. 1 @$9.95 ea.		
Family Emergency Plan, Vol. 2 @$9.95 ea.		
Family Emergency Plan, Vol. 3 @$9.95 ea.		

Please add $2.00 shipping and handling to the price of the first book ordered and $1.00 shipping for each additional book ordered in the same order. All checks or money orders must be drawn on U.S. funds, and sent with the order to: Barry Crockett, P.O. Box 1601, Orem, Utah 84059. For information on quantity discounts, please call (801) 225-8873. (Prices subject to change without notice.)

Total		
Shipping		
Total of Above		

Ship To:

Name:_____

Address: _____

City/State/Zip:_____

Country/Postal Code:_____

RECOMMENDED SUPPLIERS (1993)

BE READY
DISASTER PREPAREDNESS

Be Ready Disaster Preparedness has been recognized as one of the leading suppliers of quality emergency preparedness items. Over 2,000 different products are available with unmatched prices. Check the rest and call us last. We will not be undersold. Free catalogs also available. Be Ready Disaster Preparedness, 1405 El Camino Real #110, Oceanside, California 92054. 1-800-800-7922

EMERGENCY ESSENTIALS
RECEIVE FREE CATALOG

Features long-term storage foods, 72-hour survival kits, outdoor camping products and first aid supplies! Write Emergency Essentials, Inc., 352 North State Street, No. B, Orem, Utah 84057. Or call toll free: 1-800-999-1863.

GRAIN COUNTRY

Features controlled atmosphere packaging of cereal grains (wheat, rice, rolled oats, etc.) and legumes (beans, peas, soybeans, etc.). A moisture-barrier laminated pouch (Flexible Can™) is vacuum-sealed for extended shelf-life and inhibited bacterial growth. Grain Country also sells flour mills (hand and electric), bread-mixers, juicers, and other food preparation items. Shipping is available to all of U.S. and Canada. Ask for free information and price list. 560 W. Main, American Fork, Utah 84003 (801) 756-9516 or Toll Free: 1-800-484-4149 (ID # 8797)

K-TEC KITCHEN AND MACHINES

Wheat/Grain mills, bread mixing and food processing machines. A complete line of hand and power equipment to help you store and use whole grains everyday. Top-of-the-line hard Montana white and red storage wheat. Call Toll Free: 1-800-288-6455 or (801) 222-0888. K-TEC, 370 East 1330 South (Space G), Orem, Utah 84058 (In the Fred Meyer Shopping Plaza).

NITRO-PAK PREPAREDNESS CENTER

America's #1 source for survival foods and supplies. NITRO-PAK is well-known for their premium quality dehydrated and freeze-dried "no-cook" storage foods. They also offer a full line of 72 hour emergency kits, year supply kits, 1st aid kits, water storage containers and filters, military ready-to-eat meals (MRE's), wheat and grain mills, personal protection devices, preparedness books and videos, and much more. GUARANTEED LOWEST PRICES.

Nitro-Pak Preparedness Center (cont)

Call or write for their complete catalog—just $3 (includes a $5 discount certificate). Call Toll Free 1-800-866-4876 or (310) 802-0099, 13309 Rosecrans Ave., Dept. BC-3, Santa Fe Springs, CA 90670: FAX (310) 801-2635.

OUT N BACK
72-Hour Supply Headquarters

Complete selection of packaged 72-hour kits and Year's Supply units of air-dried and freeze-dried dehydrated foods as well as individual items for developing a supply designed just for you and your family's needs. For free monthly newsletter write or come into Out N Back, 1340 West 3500 South, Salt Lake City, UT 84119, (800) 533-7415 or Out N Back, 1797 S. State, Orem, Utah 84058. Both stores are open Monday-Saturday 10 a.m. to 6 p.m.

SAFEGUARD FOOD STORAGE &
EMERGENCY PREPAREDNESS CENTER

For free information on Food Storage, 72-Hour Kits, Water Storage, Wheat Grinders, Emergency Stoves, Lanterns, Flashlights, First Aid Kits, and other emergency products write to: Safeguard, 543 East 2100 South, Salt Lake City, UT 84106, or call 1-801-486-6001.

SALT LAKE PERMA PAK
PANTRY SUPPLY STORE

See us for our complete line of food storage, bulk grains, 72-hour kit supplies, education material. We have been satisfying customers for over 35 years. Mention this ad to find out about our free shipping offer. 230 East 6400 South, Murray, Utah 84107. (801) 268-9915 or (801) 268-9916. (Distributors of Perma Pak Food Storage & "Ready-to-Go" 72-Hour Kits.)

STAT MEDICAL SUPPLY CO.

We carry a complete line of first aid supplies and medical equipment. Save time and money using STAT as your single source supplier for your total medical supply needs. Call or write to us for our free price lists. STAT Medical Supply Co., 4555 south 300 West, Suite 500, Murray, Utah 84117. 801-261-4363.